Minority Autonomy in Western Europe

Compiled and edited by Minority Rights Group

The Minority Rights Group gratefully acknowledges all the organizations and individuals who gave financial and other assistance towards this report, including Joseph Rowntree Charitable Trust and European Human Rights Foundation.

PROFESSOR CLAIRE PALLEY is Principal of St Anne's College, Oxford. She is UK Member of the UN Sub-Commission on the Prevention of Discrimination and Protection of Minorities, and a Member of MRG's Council.

PROFESSOR ANTONY ALCOCK is Head of the Department of European Studies and Modern Languages, University of Ulster, Coleraine, Northern Ireland.

KLAUS CARSTEN PEDERSEN is Director of the Danish Foreign Policy Society, Copenhagen, Denmark.

PROFESSOR MARC BOSSUYT is Belgian Commissioner-General for Refugees and Stateless Persons and has previously served as Belgian Member of the UN Sub-Commission on the Prevention of Discrimination and Protection of Minorities.

DICK LEONARD is EC/Brussels correspondent for *The Observer*.

DR. JONATHAN STEINBERG is University Lecturer in History and Vice Master of Trinity College, Cambridge, UK.

FRED GRÜNFELD is Assistant Professor in International Relations at the Faculty of Law, University of Limburg, Maastricht, Netherlands.

British Library Cataloguing in Publication Data

A CIP catalogue record for this book is available for the British Library.

ISBN 0 946690 93 6

This report, originally titled *Co-existence in Some Plural European Societies*, was published in November 1986. This revised, updated and extended edition was published in October 1991.

Printed on bleach-free paper by Manchester Free Press

"...the recognition of the existence of regional or minority languages as an expression of cultural wealth...

...the respect of the geographical area of each regional or minority language in order to ensure that existing or new

The cover reproduces part of the text from the *Council of Europe draft European Charter for Regional and Minority Languages*, April 1991.

UNITED NATIONS COVENANT ON CIVIL AND POLITICAL RIGHTS 1966

ARTICLE 27

In those States in which ethnic, religious or linguistic minorities exist, persons belonging to such minorities shall not be denied the right, in community with the other members of their group, to enjoy their own culture, to profess and practise their own religion, or to use their own language.

CONFERENCE ON SECURITY AND CO-OPERATION IN EUROPE (CSCE), 1990.

(31) Persons belonging to national minorities have the right to exercise fully and effectively their human rights and fundamental freedoms without any discrimination and in full equality of the law.

The participating States will adopt, where necessary, special measures for the purpose of ensuring to persons belonging to national minorities full equality with the other citizens in the exercise and enjoyment of human rights and fundamental freedoms. .

(32) To belong to a national minority is a matter of a person's individual choice and no disadvantage may arise from the exercise of such choice.

Persons belonging to national minorities have the right freely to express, preserve and develop their ethnic, cultural, linguistic or religious identity and to maintain and develop their culture in all its aspects, free of any attempts at assimilation against their will. In particular, they have the right

(32.1) – to use freely their mother tongue in private as well as in public;

(32.2) – to establish and maintain their own educational, cultural and religious institutions, organizations or associations, which can seek voluntary financial and other contributions as well as public assistance, in conformity with national legislation;

(32.3) – to profess and practise their religion, including the acquisition, possession and use of religious materials, and to conduct religious educational activities in their mother tongue;

(32.4) – to establish and maintain unimpeded contacts among themselves within their country as well as contacts across frontiers with citizens of other States with whom they share a common ethnic or national origin, cultural heritage or religious beliefs;

(32.5) – to disseminate, have access to and exchange information in their mother tongue;

(32.6) – to establish and maintain organizations or associations within their country and to participate in international non-governmental organizations.

Persons belonging to national minorities can exercise and enjoy their rights individually as well as in community with other members of their group. No disadvantage may arise for a person belonging to a national minority on account of the exercise or non-exercise of any such rights.

COUNCIL OF EUROPE DRAFT EUROPEAN CHARTER FOR REGIONAL OR MINORITY LANGUAGES, 1991

ARTICLE 5

Objectives and Principles

1. Each State should, in respect of regional or minority languages, base their policies, legislation and practice on the following aims and principles:

a) the recognition of the existence of regional or minority languages as an expression of cultural wealth;

b) the respect of the geographical area of each regional or minority language in order to ensure that existing or new administrative divisions do not constitute an obstacle to the promotion of the regional or minority language in question;

c) the need for resolute action to promote regional or minority languages in order to safeguard them;

d) the elimination of all forms of discrimination concerning the use of regional or minority languages;

e) the facilitation and/or encouragement of the use of regional or minority languages, in speech and writing, in public and private life;

g) the teaching and study of regional and minority languages at all appropriate stages;

h) the provision of facilities enabling non-speakers of a regional or minority language living in the area where it is used to learn it if they so desire;

i) the promotion of study and research on regional or minority languages at universities or equivalent institutions;

j) the promotion, by appropriate measures, of mutual understanding between all the linguistic groups of the country and in particular the inclusion of respect, understanding and tolerance in relation to regional or minority languages among the objectives of education and training provided within their countries and encouragement of the mass media to pursue the same objectives;

k) the promotion of appropriate types of transnational exchanges for regional or minority languages used in identical or similar form in two or more (contracting) states.

INTRODUCTION

by Professor Claire Palley

This MRG Report is an unusual one in several respects. It was originally produced to provide some constructive and positive lessons of successful plural societies for those working to resolve the recurrent problems of Northern Ireland. In the late 1980s new political, nationalist and minority rights movements came to the fore in Eastern Europe and the USSR. European institutions such as the Council on Security and Cooperation in Europe (CSCE), the Council of Europe (CE) and the European Community (EC) have also been concerned with the rights of minorities. Today, this revised and updated Report has relevance for the new plural democracies which are emerging in Eastern Europe and the former USSR, and also for the growing numbers of pan-European institutions.

This Report is a composite one by several authors of brief case studies of minority groups in half-a-dozen countries. It presents examples of plural societies where ethnic, linguistic or religious tensions once prevailed, fuelling secessionist movements and disrupting relationships between neighbouring states. Although the risks of conflict inherent in any plural society remain, these societies now exhibit political characteristics and employ governmental arrangements which encourage amicable inter-group relationships.

MRG Reports deal with major human problems, so that, although hopeful aspects are recorded, the impression is likely to be that of pessimism. Reading several reports in sequence may even provoke the view that conflict between ethnic or religious groups cannot be reduced in plural societies. Such cynicism would be misguided. There are ways forward, even though these cannot promise overmuch; fundamental problems of social and political organization do not disappear overnight or even over a century.

Western Europe is rich in examples of accommodation within plural societies. In this context Switzerland trips from the lips. But Swiss ability to accommodate and reduce inter-group conflict is not unique in Western Europe. Nor can it be contended that its relatively successful political arrangements work only because of an unusual combination of historical and geographical factors. The Netherlands, Belgium, Finland, Italy, Denmark and Germany have also had major intercommunal problems, but have ameliorated these and exemplify societies where such divisions are currently accommodated, even if new divisions have arisen.

Obviously some examples are happier than others. The length of time their compromises have endured is longer, as in the Netherlands and Switzerland. Others have only relatively recently reached an accommodation, such as Denmark and Germany regarding their respective national minorities, Italy in the case of the South Tyrol, and Belgium. Their successes naturally stimulate questions whether these are merely the result of geographical and historical accident, or whether the experience of such states affords lessons for other plural societies where group conflict is endemic and intense.

Certain geographical factors (in the widest sense) have affected outcomes. The power and attitudes of neighbouring states are significant, especially if they place at risk peaceful co-existence of the diverse communities in neighbouring states by encouraging minorities in irredentism rather than supporting internal compromises. In this respect Sweden and Austria have shown wisdom. Again the size, characteristics and location of relatively homogenous populated areas within a state are also factors which influence whether it will hold or

fall apart or be partly merged with a neighbour. Physical barriers such as mountains and sea likewise play a part. Another crucial factor is the economy; economic growth softens inter-group competitiveness while economic decline worsens it, as demonstrated by the deterioration in Walloon-Flemish relationships with changes in industrial patterns in Belgium.

Internal political factors are, however, even more crucial. Successful plural societies operate within a democratic framework and unless there is a general respect for human rights and the rule of law, there is little respect for the rights of – sometimes unpopular – minorities. The capacity of leaders and the willingness of political parties to compromise, with majorities adopting concessive rather than majoritarian approaches and minorities accommodating rather separatist ones, are vital. Long-term integration is even possible in the presence of such factors – as in the Netherlands, where class divisions are becoming more significant than traditional religious ones.

Although political attitudes are the most important factors, it is illuminating to note[1] that institutional arrangements can play a significant part in creating a framework within which group cleavages become less sharp. This happy observation means that other societies can evaluate arrangements adopted elsewhere and adapt these (obviously with appropriate modifications) in an attempt to reduce their own inter-ethnic conflict.

The major institutional arrangements which damp down inter-group conflict are all, in lesser or greater degree, found in those plural societies dealt with in this Report. The according of a large measure of autonomy, whether political or cultural, is possibly the most significant device. Political autonomy may range from devolution of power to small communities, through regionalism, to federal government. All the societies dealt with in this Report have accorded their groups (or areas where such groups are concentrated) considerable political autonomy, either today or in the past. Such autonomy has been particularly successful in stemming separatist tendencies where there are small community units and a willingness to allow even more subdivision, as in Switzerland.

Cultural autonomy is even more necessary if there are to be harmonious inter-group relations. Threats to language and religion are potent in provoking conflict, whereas tolerance, equality and non-discrimination tend to smooth it away. However, this may not suffice and 'positive discrimination' in the sense of 'protectionism' to preserve a particular language against encroachment may be demanded, as in Belgium.

Political practices, sometimes informal but often incorporated in the constitutional structure, assist in reducing direct inter-group conflict. The adoption of proportional-representation voting systems of some kind is general. The notion of proportionality is also found in executive power-sharing arrangements, whether in informal or in institutionalized coalitions (Switzerland, Belgium and, earlier, the Netherlands). Proportionality may well be extended to a share of the spoils of public administrative office with quotas for particular ethnic groups, as in the South Tyrol.

Furthermore, to reduce the risk of divisive proposals for change, amendments of the major constitutional provisions is made difficult by requiring weighted voting in the legislature (in practice to depoliticizing issues by according mutual vetoes to the represented groups). Consultation provisions are another way of achieving this.

All these arrangements presuppose political leaders from the various communities bargaining and compromising *inter se* to maintain such systems. Even though some of these arrangements were serendipitously adopted at a time when politicians were less conscious of social and constitutional engineering, the countries described show that they are successful in assisting the maintenance of relative political stability.

If political leaders of other ethnically plural societies have the will to adopt similar practices, these are likely in the long run to blunt the edges of intergroup ethnic conflict. Of course, other cleavages, which also require tackling and which will require new skills, will then become more apparent. Every Western European society has new minorities – migrants, refugees and their descendants, some of whom are second and third generation residents (but not always citizens). The case studies of Switzerland and the Netherlands compare the similarities and differences in the treatment accorded by each, but no Western European state should be complacent while such divisions and inequalities exist unchallenged.

Footnotes

[1] These observations were first made by Professor E.A. Nordlinger writing about conflict regulation in divided societies and later elaborated by Arend Lijphart in his theory of consociational democracy.

Organization abbreviations

CE	Council of Europe
EC	European Community
EFTA	European Free Trade Association
NATO	North Atlantic Treaty Organization
UN	United Nations

ITALY – THE SOUTH TYROL
by Professor Antony Alcock

Name: Republica Italiana
Constitutional status: parliamentary democracy, president head of state
International organizations: UN, EC, CE, CSCE
Political/military alliances: NATO
Population: 57,440,000
Minorities: various ethno-linguistic minorities (see below), new minorities include Africans (especially Eritrean, Ethiopian, Somali, various north, west and central Africans). There is also a Romani (Gypsy) population. There is also large-scale immigration from southern to northern Italy.
Languages: Italian (standard plus various dialects), German (South Tyrol), French (Piedmont and elsewhere), Friulian (Friuli-Venezia-Giulia), Ladin (South Tyrol), Sard (Sardinia), Catalan (Sardinia), Slovene (Trieste, Friuli-Venezia-Giulia), Croatian, Greek, Albanian (all southern Italy).
Religion: Catholic

Italy's northernmost Province, Bolzano, otherwise known as Südtirol (South Tyrol) in German or Alto Adige in Italian, is a mountainous area bordering Austria. It contains a mixed population of 433,229 (1981 census) of which some 66% are German-speakers, 30% Italian-speakers, and 4% Ladins, speakers of an ancient Rhaeto-Romanche language.

Forced assimilation under the Fascists

South Tyrol was acquired by Italy at the end of World War I, together with the Trentino (today's Province of Trento) as part of her reward for deserting the Triple Alliance for the Triple Entente. But whereas the Province of Trento was over 95% Italian, the southern part of the Tyrol, divided from the northern part by the chain of mountains that included the Brenner Pass, was inhabited by some 85% German-speaking Austrians;[1] and thus Italy's acquisition of the area was generally incompatible with the basis upon which it was expected that peace would be made – that of the principle of self-determination.

It was specifically incompatible with the war aims of the United States, as enunciated in President Wilson's Fourteen Points, the Ninth of which stated there should be a:
'*re-adjustment of the frontiers of Italy along clearly recognizable lines of nationality*'.

Furthermore, as a great and victorious power, Italy was not obliged to sign a minority treaty governing the way she treated her new citizens of another culture, guaranteed by the League of Nations, as were the defeated powers and some of the new or re-created states of central and eastern Europe.

The Italian reason for wanting South Tyrol was to obtain a military barrier of the Brenner frontier against militant pan-Germanism, although at the Versailles conference the Italian negotiators argued that the Southern Tyrol and Trento were geographically part of Italy, and that since the area as a whole had an Italian majority then the areas as a whole should be transferred to Italy.[2]

For their part, denied the right to choose their own destiny, the South Tyrolese refused to renounce the right of self-determination and at the same time pressed for an autonomy that would enable them to live and prosper under Italy as they would no doubt have lived and prospered under Austria. If the Austro-Italian political frontier should be drawn at the Brenner, then the ethnic and cultural frontier should be drawn at the pass of Salorno, which divided South Tyrol from Trento; in other words not only the German ethnic character of the South Tyrolese but also the German ethnic character of their homeland should be respected.[3]

But if various Italian governments in the immediate post-war period were ready to recognize the right of the South Tyrolese to maintain and develop their language and culture, they had no intention of agreeing to any conditions which might close an area of presumed strategic importance to Italian economic and cultural expansion.[4] However, any dialogue on the status of the South Tyrolese within the Italian state ended with the Fascist seizure of power in 1922. Mussolini intended not only to destroy the German character of South Tyrol, but turn its people into Italians.

With these aims, a comprehensive programme of cultural genocide was carried out in the years before World War II. It included the proclamation of Italian as the only official language in the area, and therefore the dismissal of all public officials who did not speak it adequately; Italianization of place-names, public inscriptions, given names and, in some cases, family names; the institution of Italian as the only language of instruction in all schools, and the only language to be used in the courts.

The policy of cultural genocide was supported by an economic programme designed in part to alter decisively the ethnic balance in South Tyrol. Until 1934 the economy of the area was agricultural, with alpine farms and the cultivation of fruits and wines in the hands of the South Tyrolese while the Italians carried out the administration. In order to take advantage of the hydro-electric facilities of South Tyrol it was decided to set up an industrial zone outside the provincial capital, Bolzano, and a large number of Italian workers were sent there from elsewhere in the kingdom.

The South Tyrolese did not participate in the industrialization of the province. They had neither the skills nor the desire to do so, nor did the Italians intend that they should, since the zone was to be the means of increasing the Italian population. By the outbreak of World War II, 25% of the province's population was Italian.

These developments had two main effects on community relations. First, the destruction of German schools and culture and the wholesale dismissal of South Tyrolese from public offices robbed the South Tyrolese of a generation of intellectual and administrative leaders. Second, the Italian population, administrative and industrial in character, became centred in Bolzano, Merano and other smaller urban centres, with their superior housing and educational facilities, while the South Tyrolese huddled on the land. Thus the ethnic division between German and Italian was compounded by an urban-industrial/rural-agricultural divide. Average per capita income was higher among the Italians than among the South Tyrolese.[5]

Perhaps it was because the Italians knew the South Tyrolese would never abandon their cultural heritage, despite the severest pressures, that an agreement was reached in October 1939 with Nazi Germany making the South Tyrolese the object of a population transfer. Italian treatment of the South Tyrolese had caused great resentment in Germany, and also in Austria which it had taken over in the spring of 1938. But Hitler needed an Italian alliance for his aims and was determined not to let the South Tyrolese stand in his way.

Under the agreement the South Tyrolese were given the choice either of transferring to the German Reich, and thus abandoning their homeland, or of remaining in the homeland and accepting the loss of their ethnic identity under conditions of complete assimilation. The dreadful choice was not made any easier by the tremendous pressure put on them to vote for Germany. As a result over 80% did so, but the course of the war hindered the transfer process. Only about 75,000 had left by 1943 (and the Italian proportion of the population rose to 35%), and about one-third of these returned after the war.[6]

It was therefore no surprise that after the World War II the South Tyrolese were determined that the Italians should never again have a say in their future, and sought to have South Tyrol returned to Austria. To their anger and bitterness, the victorious Allies decided to leave South Tyrol with Italy. There were two reasons. One was to reward a Italy, a country that had reversed alliances for the second time in 28 years, but which would nevertheless be losing territory. The other was that the future of Austria, then under Four-Power occupation, was uncertain.

The De Gasperi-Gruber Agreement of 1946

However, in view of past experience, the Allies put pressure on the Italian and Austrian governments to come to an arrangement on the future of the South Tyrolese. At the Paris Peace Conference in September 1946, the Italian and Austrian Foreign Ministers, Alcide de Gasperi and Karl Gruber, signed the Agreement which bears their name.

Under its clauses the German-speaking inhabitants of the Province of Bolzano and the neighbouring bilingual townships of the Province of Trento were promised complete equality of rights with Italians within the framework of special provisions to safeguard their ethnic character and cultural and economic development. In addition, the populations of these zones were to be granted the exercise of autonomous legislative and executive regional power, and the framework within which this power would apply was to be drafted 'in consultation also' with local German-speaking representatives.[7]

Unfortunately, this Agreement was received in South Tyrol and in Austria with bitter disappointment. Leading Austrians and South Tyrolese insisted that the Agreement did not mean renunciation of eventual reunification of South Tyrol with Austria or renunciation of the right of the South Tyrolese to determine their own destiny.[8]

This questioning of the territorial destiny of South Tyrol was to have unfortunate effects. The Italians appreciated well enough the hatred borne them, and feared that any South Tyrolese attempt to repair the economic, social and cultural ravages of Fascism would be at the expense of the province's Italian community, so that any weakening or even reduction of the Italian population would be but a prelude to calls for a referendum on the return of South Tyrol to Austria in an area where the cultural minority was still, nevertheless, a majority, followed by pressure in international fora to that end.

The Autonomy Statute of 1948

The result was that the Autonomy Statute granted the Province of Bolzano in 1948[9] as fulfilment of the De

Gasperi-Gruber Agreement was very restricted, following a minimal consultation with the South Tyrolese in its drafting.

It provided for the restoration to the South Tyrolese of their German cultural identity through the re-establishment of German-language schools which were to be separate from Italian schools, the right to use German in relations with public offices, and the return of German names that had been Italianized. However, it contained nothing about the restoration of the German character of South Tyrol and it was quite clear that the cultural, economic and social development of the South Tyrolese would remain in Italian hands.

This was achieved in three main ways. The first was simply not to endow the Province of Bolzano, and its South Tyrolese majority in the population that would presumably be reflected in the Provincial Assembly, with any meaningful powers, and certainly none regarding the economic development of the province.

Secondly, the South Tyrol was placed with the Province of Trento within the larger framework of a Trentino-Alto Adige Region. It was the Region that possessed not only more powers but also all the most important powers, including those relating to agriculture, tourism and industrial development. But since the Province of Trento was more populous than Bolzano, and since Trento was 99% Italian and Bolzano 33% Italian, the Regional Assembly was dominated by a two-thirds Italian majority.

Thirdly, since Italy was not a federal state but a centralized state with power devolved to the regions, government approval had to be given to any regional or provincial legislation before these could take effect. This approval might also require the prior issue of so-called 'Executive Measures', cabinet decrees having the force of law, whose function was to co-ordinate the legislative and administrative powers of the regions and provinces with the State, including defining their respective spheres of interest in the matter. This procedure was cumbersome and often lengthy, and what made it even more exasperating was that if the province had the legislative powers to deal with a matter, such as housing, it was the state that provided – or did not provide – the finance.

There were other ways too in which a restrictive view was taken of the autonomy. For example, the De Gasperi-Gruber Agreement's stated aim of bringing about ethnic proportions in public offices was interpreted not to mean a blanket two-thirds: one-third distribution of posts in all provincial, state and semi-state bodies operating in the province but only to offices of the provincial administration.

However, there was one feature of government where power-sharing was institutionalized between the two main ethnic groups, not only at provincial and regional but also district council level. This required the governments of the Region and the Province of Bolzano, ie., President, Vice-Presidents and Assessors responsible for the various sectors, as well as the governments of the 116 district councils in South Tyrol, to be composed of representatives from both groups in their respective proportions.[10]

But did the obligation of both groups to participate in the government mean that there should be a coalition government policy? In other words, if the Italians had a right to be represented in the South Tyrol provincial government administration, was there an obligation for the South Tyrolese to devise a common programme with them? In fact, such a coalition has almost always existed, even though it might take some time to put together.

What has made matters easier is that the South Tyrolese are overwhelmingly represented by the *Südtiroler Volkspartei* (SVP), which is close in ideology to the Italian Christian Democratic Party, and thus although the Italian ethnic vote is always split between the traditional political parties covering the whole range of the political spectrum, coalition partners are available, and, reflecting coalitions at national level, the Italian Social Democratic and Socialist parties have also participated in the provincial government. Nevertheless should the SVP, with its clear majority over all other parties, decide on a policy with which the Italian members of the coalition do not agree, there is nothing to prevent the Provincial Assembly adopting that policy by the usual democratic process of majority vote.

Before the revision of the Autonomy Statute in 1972 this was not particularly important, since the number of sectors in which the Provincial Assembly could act was few, they were mostly unimportant, and the state had the last word through Executive Measures and the provision of finance and thus the will of the democratic majority could be thwarted in most matters. But there was another safeguard, namely that laws that were held to violate the principle of equality between the two language groups – but only such laws – could be contested before the Constitutional Court, although before 1972 only the Region could contest state laws and thus the South Tyrolese had to rely on Italian support in the Region to take such action on their behalf if desired.[11] On occasion this support was not forthcoming.

By the 1950s South Tyrolese dissatisfaction with the 1948 Autonomy Statute and its application had led to the first acts of violence, initially aimed at breaking the grip of the Region and having its powers transferred in order to provide a meaningful autonomy for the Province of Bolzano.

It was clear that the manner in which the autonomy was being applied was blocking the social mobility of the South Tyrolese during a period when there was a massive flight from the agricultural sector requiring the creation of new jobs in the countryside and towns, housing to accommodate job and population shifts, and increased vocational training facilities. Failure to respond to the pressures involved risked causing emigration of South Tyrolese from their homeland to seek work in Austria or West Germany, thus weakening the solidarity of the group, or immigration of skilled Italian workers to take jobs in expanding industry and commerce, thus upsetting further the ethnic balance in the province.

However, in May 1955 the Four-Power occupation of Austria ended, and the Austrian State Treaty was signed, restoring that country's independence and conferring on it a status of permanent neutrality. Article 5 of the Treaty laid down the frontiers of Austria as being those of 1 January 1938. Guaranteeing, as signatories, those frontiers, the United States, the USSR, the UK and France made it clear that a return of South Tyrol to Austria was no longer a possibility, and thus confirmed, after 10 years of doubt, the territorial destiny of South Tyrol as part of the Italian state.

Nevertheless, terrorism in South Tyrol did continue for another decade and a half, involving later pan-German and neo-Nazi forces from Austria and West Germany. Austria brought the South Tyrol question before the United Nations in 1960 and 1961,[12] alleging that Italy had not correctly fulfilled the De Gasperi-Gruber Agreement. The international pressures (from the UN and the Council of Europe) to resolve the situation, coupled with the knowledge that concessions to the South Tyrolese would not be merely the first steps to secession, led to intense negotiations between Rome and Bolzano on the one hand, and Rome and Vienna on the other.

The Improved Autonomy Package of 1972

The result was a package agreed in 1969, under which the South Tyrol would receive a greatly improved autonomy, and Italy obtained from Austria a promise that when all the measures due under the new autonomy had been implemented, the latter would give a declaration regarding the end of the conflict.[13]

But if the territorial destiny of South Tyrol had been accepted by both Austria and Italy, was it accepted by the South Tyrolese? The answer to this question must be given in two parts. On the one hand, while the territorial destiny of South Tyrol was in doubt, while the economic and social position of the South Tyrolese people was so uncertain, while terrorism and the actions of the Italian security forces created a gulf between the South Tyrolese and Italian people, it was not surprising that the overwhelming mass of South Tyrolese were in favour of a return to Austria.

But once the question of the frontier ceased to be relevant, once the gains of the improved Autonomy Statute began to be felt, once terrorism and security activity ceased, the South Tyrolese changed their minds completely. Instead of being poor relations in their homelands, they were now the rulers of a rich province that made an envious contrast to the bankruptcies, unemployment, decay and political disorder in other areas of Italy. The maintenance of their cultural characteristics and the solidarity of the group were assured, to the extent that it was in their own hands. And many thought it was surely preferable, as Italian citizens, to be part of the EEC and NATO rather than an small, neutral and relatively isolated European country like Austria.

On the other hand, the South Tyrolese people were massively represented by the SVP which regularly took 90% of the German ethnic vote and it was stated in the statutes of the SVP that, although it considered that the right of self-determination for the South Tyrolese people was inalienable, the party recognized the De Gasperi-Gruber Agreement as 'the basis for the national development of the Tyrolese minority *within the Italian state*'.[14] However there appeared to be a contradiction between agreement to operate within the Italian state and the acceptance that the exercise of self-determination might lead to separation from that state.

Traditionally the call for self-determination has indeed been associated with the demand for separation, either of a whole people or of an ethnic or linguistic minority from the host state. But the right of self-determination has recently been re-interpreted to mean the right of a people or group to decide freely what legislative and administrative powers in the cultural, and, possibly other fields, it might be necessary to obtain to enable it to maintain its cultural characteristics and separate identity. Separation would then only be sought as a last resort if the state denied these legitimate demands.[15]

The principal features of the improved autonomy,[16] which came into force in 1972 through amendment of the 1948 statute were:

a) that if the Region continued to exist, the Province of South Tyrol would have transferred to its jurisdiction legislative and administrative powers in regard to a large number of sectors hitherto controlled by the Region and the Italian state, including agriculture and tourism;

b) the principle of ethnic proportions which had hitherto applied only to employment in offices of the provincial administration was extended to apply to all state and semi-state bodies operating in the Province, with the exception of the Ministry of Defence and the various police forces, but competence in both languages was required, through examination, for entry, preparation or transfer, at every grade from chauffeur or caretaker through to director;

c) in regard to finance the Province receives nine-tenths of the taxes raised there as well as a proportionate share of the state health budget and state grants earmarked for the special development programme of the regions;[17]

d) the Province could contest state laws before the Constitutional Court;[18]

e) in regard to decision-making, it was spelt out that if a provincial bill was held to violate the equality of rights of one language group, a majority of the deputies of that language group could call for a vote by language groups. If the bill was passed despite the adverse vote of two-thirds of the deputies of the language group that called for the vote, that group could contest the law before the Constitutional Court. While the appeal was in progress the law adopted remained in force.[19]

In South Tyrol the question of ethnic identity was very important. It governed the school to which a child should go, access to employment in the public administration at all levels, the allocation of public housing and even the candidature of those standing for election. Everyone in the province was now required to make an official declaration at the time of the national census as to his or her ethnic group, with parents making the declaration on behalf of their children and these declarations could not be disputed by the authorities.[20]

Effects of the Autonomy Package

Within less than two decades of the implementation of the improved autonomy statute (although in some areas the package had not yet been completely implemented), political and economic relations in the province had been transformed, particularly to the advantage of the South Tyrolese.

The South Tyrolese were enabled to begin the process of being represented throughout the administration of their homeland at all levels, crucial not only in terms of jobs and pensions but of morale. Administration expanded rapidly as the Provincal Assembly not only took over sectors and powers from the Region but received considerable financial support to implement policy.

There was a tremendous economic boom, led by tourism, and aided by the relative decline of the lira compared to the Germanic currencies, and the completion of the Brenner motorway. To meet the demand nine new ski areas were developed, so that tourism in South Tyrol approached an all-year-round activity. The provincial government not only loaned money for guest-houses to be equipped with modern facilities, but arranged to pay a sizeable proportion of the interest on bank loans for the modernization or building of new hotels and guest-houses. The result was a construction boom.

The money entering the province through tourism was added to the considerable sums accruing to the province through its receipt of 1.61% of sectoral government expenditures, as well as sums received from the EC's Common Agricultural Policy, particularly from price support and farm modernization measures applying in mountainous areas.

The most important problem became the decline of the Italian group in terms of numbers and morale. The economic boom had benefited the South Tyrolese to a much greater extent, and the Italian-dominated industrial sector was marked by unemployment, inflation, stagnation and bankruptcy. Public administration was also affected. In order to reach true ethnic proportions by the year 2002, as required by the 1972 Autonomy Statute,[21] the number of Italians in state and semi-state bodies would have to be reduced over the years by over 2700.

An indication of the seriousness of this situation in regard to employment in the Italian community was that Italians began to declare themselves or their children as Germans (ie. South Tyrolese), thus raising the spectre of South Tyrolese assimilation of Italians rather than what the Autonomy Statute had been designed to prevent, namely Italian assimilation of South Tyrolese. Whether it was because of such declarations, or that the economic situation had led to Italians leaving the province, it was of considerable concern to Italian nationalists that the Italian presence in South Tyrol declined from 33.3% according to the 1971 census, to 30% according to that of 1981, and is expected to fall further by the census of 1991.

A second serious problem was that of those who either would not or could not give the declaration as to their ethnic group. There were those, such as children of mixed marriages, who might genuinely be unable to decide which group they belonged to. Others, on the other hand, alarmed at the potential loss of rights that might occur following failure to give the declaration, argued that it was unconstitutional to have to make such a declaration as it violated Article 3 of the Italian Constitution which provided for equality of rights for all citizens without distinction as to sex, race, language, religion or political belief.

At the time of the 1980 local council elections three candidates of the New Left Party were disqualified, one for declaring himself both German and Italian; the second for declaring that she belonged to no group; and the third for declaring himself Slovene.[22] In 1984 the Council of State declared the law requiring the declaration illegal because it did not provide the opportunity for citizens to declare themselves as 'other language' or 'mixed language'.[23]

Negotiations took place in 1991 for a reorganization of the language group survey for the 1991 census. The South Tyrolese had proposed that every inhabitant of South Tyrol should be able to give a true declaration as to their linguistic membership (ie. German, Italian, Ladin or other), but that means for the three recognized linguistic groups to maintain their claim for protective and preferential measures should continue in force, in particular that the declaration should take two forms, one for statistical purposes and the other for maintenance of the system of ethnic proportions.[24] This has

been accepted.[25]

A third problem concerned the unexpected failure of sufficient numbers of South Tyrolese to apply for posts in state and semi-state bodies and get them. Such factors as the language examination, housing shortages in Bolzano, competition from the expanding provincial administration and the tourist boom played their part. The result was a crisis in some organizations, particularly the railways and postal services. According to the Executive Measures implementing the Package, the service concerned could take on staff from elsewhere in Italy on temporary contracts but only for a twelve-month period, non-renewable. Even this had not sufficed, and Italian politicians and trade unions protested that it was absurd for job vacancies to remain unfulfilled in the province in large numbers while unemployment was high elsewhere in Italy.[26]

Unresolved issues

The existence of these sorts of problems has meant that if the political situation cannot be compared to the years of intercommunity bitterness and terrorism of the late 1950s and the 1960s, nevertheless there are grounds for some unease.

First there is the decline in the numbers of the Italian group, expected to be confirmed by the October 1991 census. This decline has led to calls in many quarters in Italy for a revision of the 1972 Autonomy Statute. More seriously it lead to a spectacular showing by the neo-fascist *Movimento Sociale Italiano* (MSI) at the 1984 local elections, when it became the largest political party in the Bolzano City Council. The policy of the MSI is the abolition of the Autonomy Statute.

But the rise of the MSI brings with it another threat. Should the MSI become the sole or major representative of the Italian community in the Provincial Assembly, how will it be possible to continue one of the pillars of the system of political accommodation in the province, namely power-sharing, if on the one hand there are no Italian deputies willing to share power with South Tyrolese deputies, and on the other, if there is no agreement between the communities about the framework within which power is to be shared.

On the other hand, there are still some South Tyrolese who are dissatisfied at the slow Italian implementation of the package, who see the 1984 Council of State decision as the first step in the eventual dismantling of the autonomy and proof that Italy cannot be relied upon, and who believe that a fundamental injustice was done in 1919 that can only be repaired by the separation of South Tyrol from Italy. To all of these, if South Tyrol cannot return to Austria, the transformation of the Province into a Free State, or San Marino status within Italy, is a very attractive alternative.[27]

Third, if only four of the 137 measures of the Package now remain to be fulfilled,[28] and their implementation is not expected to take much longer, that fulfilment will also bring to the front Austria's obligation to give a formal declaration regarding the end of the conflict. However the nature of this declaration is controversial. According to the Italians the declaration is to relate to the closing of the South Tyrol question.[29] According to the Austrians and the SVP, the declaration is to relate to the closing of the dispute about the fulfilment of the De Gasperi-Gruber Agreement.[30]

The issue here is a subtle but not unimportant one. The

Italian thesis is that the provisions of the Package are not part of the De Gasperi-Gruber Agreement but additional measures granted freely. The Austrian thesis is that the Package made up the gaps and inadequacies of the 1948 Autonomy Statute. Austria and the SVP had wanted the Package provisions to be internationally guaranteed, so that if any were revoked by Rome, Vienna could take the matter before the International Court at the Hague.

If the Austrian thesis should prevail, then any revocation of all or part of it could be brought before the International Court for failure to implement an international agreement. But if the Italian thesis were accepted, then the Court would first have to decide whether the Package was part of the Agreement or additional to it.[31] If the latter, the scope for manoeuvre of the Austrian government would be limited accordingly, and South Tyrolese fears about the future would not be allayed, especially if Rome is seen to come under nationalist pressure following dissatisfaction with the effects of the Autonomy Statute on the Italian community.

Fourth, the dynamic development of the EC has brought in its train problems for South Tyrol, and particularly the system of ethnic proportions in public employment. In relation to Article 48 of the Treaty of Rome governing freedom of movement and particularly its clause iv on the applicability of the Article to the civil service, the European Court of Justice ruled that it was necessary to ensure that the effectiveness and scope of the provisions of the Treaty on Freedom of Movement of Workers and Equality of Treatment of Nationals of all Member States should not be restricted by interpretations of the concept of public service which were based on domestic law alone and which might obstruct the application of Community rules.[32]

Furthermore, posts in the civil service were defined as those which put the holders thereof in the position of participating directly in the exercise of official authority or of making use of prerogatives in the nature of powers conferred by public law in regard to members of the public:

The duties must involve acts of will which affect private individuals by requiring their obedience or, in the event of disobedience, by compelling them to comply. To make a list... is practically impossible, but certainly the first examples which come to mind are posts which involve the exercise of powers relating to policing, defence of the state, the administration of justice and assessments to tax.[33]

The effect of the rulings of the European Court of Justice is therefore to remove from Member States the right to define what constitutes the civil service, and therefore posts in it. The object, of course, was to ensure that Member States did not thwart freedom of movement by declaring certain occupations part of the civil service, and thus excluded to foreigners. The railways in Belgium, the nursing profession in France, teacher-training in Germany, and scientific work in Italian research laboratories have been some areas specifically affected by later rulings of the Court.[34]

However, in South Tyrol, the system of ethnic proportions extended to the state railways and the nursing profession, while teachers were employed in the schools of their ethnic group. Furthermore the concept of public employment covered all grades working in the administration concerned including gardeners, secretaries, chauffeurs, janitors and kitchen staff.

If Italy is now not able to say who or what is a civil servant,

then of the some 29,000 posts in the public administration in the Province subject to the system of ethnic proportions, probably less than 2000 can be described as being held by persons participating directly in the exercise of official authority, and competition for vacancies will be far more open so that the composition of the various administrations may cease to reflect the ethnic proportions in the Province.

This would mean a formidable breach in a system designed to defuse ethnic tension by ensuring, on the one hand, that the ethnic minority is seen to be participating in the administration of the homeland where it is the numerical majority, while at the same time the ethnic majority is able to maintain a vital presence in a part of the state where it is the numerical minority.[35]

For example, language would become an even more important factor in obtaining an administrative job in South Tyrol. But if the job description required a certain level of competence in both German and Italian, since the South Tyrolese tended to know Italian better than Italians knew German, there might be a risk that administrations would be dominated by South Tyrolese, thus adding to Italian discontentment.

The seriousness of the situation led to a special visit to the European Commission in Brussels by South Tyrolese leaders in November 1990.[36]

Some lessons

The South Tyrol question, with its long history, contains one of the richest stores of information in the world on the issues involved in dealing with the problems of divided communities and the success or failure of the techniques used – in this case provincial autonomy. The South Tyrolese have been eager to put their experience at the disposal of other areas in the world with comparable problems.

One lesson is that of the importance of a stable political framework – both internally and internationally. Both the Austrian and Italian governments have shown themselves determined not to let the South Tyrol question make difficulties between them, and the operation of the autonomy has been recognized by the South Tyrolese leaders as providing a very positive change in the fortunes of the group.

With Austria expected to join the EC without difficulty after 1992, thus adding to the number of federal or regional-type states in it, the South Tyrolese have taken the lead in advocating a future integrated Europe based on the regions rather than the states. This policy also has the considerable advantage of uniting pro- and anti-Package South Tyrolese and Italians eager to distance themselves from Rome-based centralization.[37] It also supports an ideal of self-determination which encompasses political structures other than that of separation, which would only be sought as a last resort if the state denied legitimate demands of territorial minorities.

Furthermore, provincial economic autonomy has been supported by the automatic receipt of a fixed quota of the national sectorial budget. Not only does this provide a sizable and stable amount, which facilitates planning, but which also aids its distribution to further the aims of the different communities. These lessons from South Tyrol are important not only for Western but also for Eastern Europe, as their many and varied peoples come to determine their destinies.

Footnotes

1. Alcock, A, *History of the South Tyrol Question*, London, Michael Joseph, 1970, (hereinafter *History*), Table D, p.496.
2. *Ibid.*, pp.20-21.
3. The programme of the *Deutscher Verband*, a union of all the German-speaking political parties in the area, in *ibid.*, pp.27-30.
4. *Ibid.*, pp.30-31.
5. *Ibid.*, pp.33-45, and Table D, p.496.
6. The Options Agreement and its implementation is discussed in *ibid.*, pp. 45-59.
7. Text of the De Gasperi-Gruber Agreement in *ibid.*, Appendix 1, pp.473-474.
8. *Ibid.*, pp.138-40.
9. Test of the Autonomy Statute, Constitutional Law of 20 February 1948, n.5, in *ibid.*, Appendix 2, pp.475-492.
10. Autonomy Statute, Articles 30, 44, 54.
11. Autonomy Statute, Article 83.
12. Alcock, *op.cit.*, pp.330-349, and pp.373-377.
13. Text of the Package Agreement in *ibid.*, pp.434-449 and in Alcock., A., *Südtirol seit dem Paket*, Vienna, Braumuller, 1982, (hereinafter *Paket*), Annex 2, pp.209-237.
14. Alcock, *Paket*, p.164.
15. Professor Theodor Veiter in *Das Menschenrecht*, Vienna, April 1970, p.12. Veiter's claim that acceptance of the 1969 Package Agreement by the SVP at a special party congress amounted to exercise of the right of self-determination by the South Tyrolese has been disputed, principally on the grounds that the South Tyrolese were not consulted directly in a referendum, and since the SVP did not represent *all* South Tyrolese, and the vote in favour of the Agreement at the Congress was very close (52.9%), it was not certain that the Agreement did gain the support of a majority of the South Tyrolese – or indeed the Ladin community. Alcock, *Paket*, pp.165-6.
16. D.P.R. of 13/8/72, n.670.
17. Volgger, F., *South Tyrol – an Introduction*, Bolzano, Provincial Government Publication, 1989. The system was changed in the mid-1980s. Until then Article 78 of the 1972 Autonomy Statute had been interpreted to mean that the Province should automatically receive 1.6% of any state expenditure in all the important and relevant sectors of the economy and social welfare. The percentage of 1.61% was reached by adding the percentage of the provincial population to the national population (0.76%) to the percentage of the provincial territory to the national territory (2.46%), and dividing by two.
18. D.P.R. n.670, Article 98.
19. D.P.R. n.670, Article 92.
20. D.P.R. of 26 July 1976, n.752, Article 18.
21. *Ibid.*, Article 46.
22. These issues discussed fully in Alcock, *Paket*, pp.65-69.
23. Decision of 17/4/84, n.439.
24. *Volksbote* (Bolzano), 2/5/91.
25. D.L. of 1 August 1991, No 253.
26. *Alto Adige* (Bolzano), 16/9/76.
27. Alcock, *Paket*, p.167, and in issues of the Südtiroler Heimatbund (SHB), *Heimatbote* (Bolzano) 1984, 1985, etc.
28. *Volksbote* (Bolzano), 2/5/91.
29. Communique of the Press Office of the Presidency of the Council of Ministers, 13/5/88.
30. Alcock, *Paket*, pp.20-28.
31. *Ibid.*, p.23.
32. European Court of Justice (ECJ), *Commission v Belgium*, case 149/79, Court Reports (CR) 1980, p.3882.
33. ECJ, *Sotgiu v Deutsche Bundespost*, case 152/73, CR 1974, pp.1731-2.
34. ECJ, *Commission v Belgium*, case 149/79; *Commission v France*, case 307/84; *Commission v Baden-Wurttemberg*, case 66/85; *Commission v Italy*, case 225/85.
35. These issues discussed in Alcock, A., 'Proportional Representation in Public Employment as a technique for diminishing conflict in culturally divided communities: The Case of South Tyrol', in *Regional Politics and Policy*, vol. 1, no 1, 1991, London, Cass, pp.74-86.
36. *Volksbote* (Bolzano), 29/11/90.
37. *Volksbote* (Bolzano), 22/11/90, 30/5/91.

FINLAND – THE SWEDISH-SPEAKING COMMUNITY
by Professor Antony Alcock

Name: Suomen Tasavalta
Constitutional status: parliamentary democracy, president head of state
International organizations: UN, Nordic Union, EFTA, CE, CSCE
Political/military alliances: neutral
Area: 338,130 sq. km.
Population: 4,975,000. (1989)
Minorities: Swedish speakers (6%) of population
Languages: Finnish, Swedish
Religion: Lutheran Evangelical Church (official religion)

Just over 297,000 or 6% of the population of Finland are Swedish-speaking Finish citizens. Some 22,900 inhabit the Åland Islands, where they form 95% of the population. The Åland Islands enjoy a special autonomous system of government, and the situation of the two groups needs separate analysis.

The Swedes on mainland Finland

The Swedes came to Finland in the course of crusades in the 12th Century and began a long domination of the country, incorporating it into Sweden until forced to cede it to Russia in 1809. During that time the Swedish language and culture prevailed among all classes and in government, business, education and the courts. Even after the cession of Finland to Russia the country continued to be administered by Swedes. The re-emergence of the Finnish language in the late 19th Century resulted in the privileged position of Swedish being moderated in 1902 in favour of a system of equality between the two languages.[1]

A few weeks after the Bolshevik Revolution of 1917 the Finns declared their independence. In the Finnish Constitution, promulgated in 1919, both Finnish and Swedish were proclaimed as national languages, with citizens entitled to use either language before the courts or the administration, and all official acts, bills and orders had to be published in both languages.

Today the Swedish-speaking population of mainland Finland is concentrated in two areas, along the southern coast between Helsinki and Hangö, and along the western coast between Pori and Jakobstad.

There are two consequences of the declaration of the equality of two languages. First, there has been no need for legislation providing for special protection of the Swedish minority, such as, for example, linguistic proportions in public employment.

Second, communal boundaries have been drawn to make them as nearly unilingual as possible.[2] Communes are declared bilingual wherever the minority exceeds 8% of the population or contains at least 3000 persons from the minority. There are 24 communes that are unilingually Swedish, 20 with a Swedish majority and 21 where the minority is Swedish.[3]

With regard to education, Swedish-speaking children go to their own primary, secondary and vocational schools. In 1990 there were 321 Swedish primary schools with an enrolment of some 31,200 out of a total of 4466 primary schools with an overall enrolment of some 568,000. There were 31 Swedish secondary schools out of 447, with 4900 pupils out of an overall enrolment of 92,600.[4] Communes are obliged to set up primary schools for the minority wherever there are at least 13 pupils from that minority.

In order to maintain higher education in Swedish there is one Swedish-language university in Finland – the Åbo Akademi University in Åbo/Turku. The Swedish School of Higher Education in Trade and Commerce is situated in Helsinki. A number of courses in Swedish are also given at the University of Helsinki, with the right to use the language in examinations.

There are four main Swedish daily newspapers, one of which is amongst the largest in the country in terms of sales. There are about 10 others – local papers, dailies, weeklies, etc. There is a daily Swedish-language radio programme and programmes in Swedish appear on television.

At the political level, a Swedish political party, the Swedish People's Party is represented in the Finnish Parliament, and it is estimated that about 75% of the Swedish-speaking population votes for it, mainly for cultural reasons. It has participated in various post-war coalition governments.

There can be little doubt that the Swedish community in Finland has been treated very satisfactorily, in administrative and material terms. Yet no guarantees exist on the Finnish mainland for the maintenance of Swedish, although after World War I the idea of an autonomous administration for those areas where Swedish predominated was canvassed, without, however, finding much support in either group.[5]

The only problem for the minority is the decline of the Swedish-speaking community in absolute and relative terms. In 1920 nearly 339,000 persons, 11% of the Finnish population, claimed Swedish as their mother-tongue.[6] Since then the decline has been relentless, and a cause of great concern. Among the reasons given are the lower birth-rate of the group (17.9 per thousand as against 21.5 for the Finns), mixed marriages, and emigration.[7] This situation contrasts strongly with that on the Åland Islands where the Finnish government has undertaken to maintain both Swedish and the Swedish character of the Islands.

The Swedes of the Åland Islands

As with the rest of Finland, the Islands, which were entirely Swedish-speaking, were ceded to Russia in 1809. Russia particularly wanted the Islands since they had a strategic value, dominating the approaches to Stockholm, the Gulf of Bothnia, and the Gulf of Finland with its approaches to St Petersburg.

Shortly after obtaining the Islands, Russia fortified them, but these fortifications were destroyed in 1854 by British and French troops during the Crimean War. Although not engaged in the war, Sweden claimed the Islands back during peace discussions held at Paris in 1856. This claim was unsuccessful, but Russia was forced to accede to a Convention providing for demilitarization in an Appendix to the 1856 Paris Peace Treaty.[8]

After the declaration of Finnish independence in 1917, the Islanders, fearing possible threats to their Swedish language and culture, sought reunification with Sweden. And that country too wanted the Islands for strategic reasons against a Russian state potentially far more dangerous than that of the Tsars.[9]

During the peace negotiations at Versailles in 1919 after World War I, Sweden asked the Allied Powers for a plebiscite to decide the future of the Islands, along the lines of that proposed for North Slesvig, lost by Denmark following the 1864 war with the German Confederation.[10]

The Finnish government, hoping that a far-reaching autonomy in favour of the Islanders would induce them to drop demands for reunification with Sweden, argued that the issue was a domestic problem and therefore for Finland alone to settle, and began drafting a Statute of Autonomy for the Islands. The Statute was promulgated in 1920, the year the British Foreign Secretary brought the Åland Islands question before the Council of the League of Nations.

A legal committee of the League decided that in international law the question was not a purely domestic Finnish affair, and the question of the territorial destiny of the Islands was then submitted to another committee of the League, which reported in April 1921, that since the Islanders represented less than 10% of the Swedish population of Finland, they could not claim the right of self-determination which applied to national groups as a whole. It recommended that Finland should have sovereignty over the Islands but that special guarantees on the Islands' language and culture should be provided and that the Islands should remain demilitarized.

Two months later, on 24 June 1921, the Council of the League endorsed these recommendations, urging Finland and Sweden to negotiate on the issues concerned and stating that the League would guarantee any solution reached. On 27 June 1921 an agreement was reached between Finland and Sweden, according to which the former undertook to preserve the Swedish language, culture and traditions of the Islanders and to introduce measures to maintain the Swedish character of the Islands, and to forward to the League any complaints from the Islanders about the way the measures concerned were being applied. For its part, in accepting the decision of the Council of the League of 24 June, Sweden automatically withdrew its claim to sovereignty over the Islands.[11]

The Finnish government thereupon amended the 1920 Autonomy Statute so as to incorporate the guarantees requested, and the revised statute, commonly known as the Åland Guarantee Act, was accepted by the Islanders in 1922.

Relations between Finland, Sweden and the Åland Islands developed satisfactorily between the wars, but a number of technical shortcomings in the Act as well as demands by the Islanders to extend its scope led to pressure for revision. Work, however, was interrupted by World War II, during which the USSR attacked Finland, which led, after a short period of peace, to Finland later fighting on the side of Germany. This had an effect after the war on the revision of the Autonomy Statute, which as a result was not completed until 1951.[12]

The new Autonomy Act, containing 45 articles, came into force on 1 January 1952.[13] It is this Act which not only gives the Islanders almost absolute control of their own affairs but enables the Swedish character of their homeland to be preserved.

Autonomy provisions

The basic principle of the autonomy is that the Islanders have the right to control their own affairs subject only to the maintenance of Finland as a state. The Islands, which collectively enjoy the status of a province of Finland, have a single-chamber parliament of 27 members. The administration is in the hands of a seven-member Provincial Executive Council. The members of the Council are appointed by parliament but the chairman, who is the Governor of the Islands, must have his appointment agreed by the Finnish government.

In conducting its legislative business the Islands' parliament either issues laws independently in the fields in which it has competence, or adopts analogous national laws for implementation in the Islands, either in their original form or with the appropriate changes. The laws issued by the Islands' parliament can only be ratified by the President of the Republic. He has three months in which to approve or veto such laws, and the veto can only be exercised on two grounds – that the Islands' parliament has exceeded its competence, or that the law in question threatens the security of the state. On the other hand, before the Finnish government issues administrative orders which are to apply solely to the Islands but which relate to matters in the jurisdiction of the state, the Provincial Executive Council must be consulted.

Article 13 of the Autonomy Act lists the 21 fields in which the provincial parliament enjoys legislative power. Among the most important of these are the right to expropriate property in the public interest; education (but parliament must observe national principles on age and standards of competence of students); communal administration; taxation; electoral law (but Finnish laws on the voting age must be respected); labour exchanges; housing; agriculture and fisheries; the police and maintenance of public order and security; commerce and industry, including planning and building regulations; health and hospital services (but with the obligation to respect national regulations regarding the qualifications of medical staff and the combating of human and animal epidemics.)

The Provincial parliament determines the Islands' budget. Revenue is raised from income and corporation taxes, customs duties and licences. The rates of these are, however, fixed by the national government which also collects them before paying them back to the Islands. But the Islands can impose supplementary and temporary income taxes. (Art. 23).

Justice in the Province is administered by national law courts (Art. 21). Although the Islanders are exempt from military service, on the grounds that the demilitarization of the Islands is still in force, those eligible have to serve for a comparable period in the pilotage or lighthouse service or in another section of the civil service (Art. 34).

The Swedish character of the Islanders and their homeland is preserved through four means: regulations on language; education; regional citizenship; and the acquisition of property on the Islands. With regard to language, Swedish was declared the official language of the Islands, although a Finnish-speaker may use his language before the courts. Swedish must be used in official correspondence between the provincial administration and the state authorities operating in the Province, as well as between the two of them on the one hand and the Finnish government and organs of the state authorities and courts which include the Islands in their administrative districts on the other. No one may be employed in the Islands' civil service who cannot prove full command of Swedish in speech and writing (Arts. 36-39).

In education the teaching language is Swedish. Neither the Provincial Parliament nor the communes are obliged to maintain any schools in which the teaching language is not Swedish. Instruction may not be given in a language other than Swedish without the consent of the commune concerned (Art. 35). The population of the Islands enjoys Åland regional citizenship, the qualification for which is an unbroken period of five years' residence in the Province. Regional citizenship may be acquired by marriage, but only when a woman marries a man already in possession of such citizenship. Residence outside the Province for a period of five years entails loss of regional citizenship.

Only those with regional citizenship can acquire land in the Islands or vote in communal and provincial elections. In order to carry on a business in the Province persons must have regional citizenship or been resident and domiciled there for at least five years. Companies, partnerships, etc., may only have their legal headquarters in the Province if all their board members have regional citizenship or been domiciled there for at least five years. However, the Provincial Executive Council may grant permission for firms or individuals to set up in business if it feels so inclined.

If ownership of property is transferred by means other than inheritance or expropriation to a person who does not possess regional citizenship, or to a firm whose legal headquarters are not in the Province, then the Province, the commune, or a private individual with regional citizenship – in that order – have the right to redeem the property. Any disputes between the acquisitor and redeemer as to the purchase price must be settled in court. However, the Provincial Executive Council does have the power to waive these conditions (Arts. 3-5).

Finally, the provisions of the Autonomy Statute may not be amended or abolished without the consent of the Provincial Parliament (Art. 44).

A new Autonomy Act has been adopted in 1991. The Act will apparently come into force in 1993. The main aims behind the revision of the Autonomy Act were to fix the borders of legislative competence between the Åland Parliament and the Parliament of Finland, to transfer more sectors of legislation to the Åland Parliament, and to provide a framework for freer economic action within the autonomy system. Examples of new legislation and administrative spheres which are transferred to Åland by the new act are legislation concerning the use of Åland's own flag, social welfare in its entirety, rent legislation, postal and radio services and certain sectors of alcohol legislation.

Some lessons

The position of the Swedish-speaking population of Finland has been generally considered as one of the most sympathetic and accommodating given to a minority group by a state. What, if any, are the lessons for other European states?

The main lesson, as in the case of South Tyrol, is that the issue of territorial destiny is crucial. On the mainland, Swedes are considered and see themselves not as a cultural minority but as co-founders of the Finnish state. For their part the Åland Islanders enjoy an extraordinary degree of autonomy in an area where they are such an overwhelming majority precisely because Sweden withdrew its claim to the Islands in 1921, and has refrained from pursuing it since.

In this regard the events of 1945 are instructive. At the close of World War II the destiny of Finland itself was at stake following defeat at the hands of the USSR. Incorporation into the USSR like the Baltic Republics on the other side of the Gulf of Finland or satellite status in the Soviet sphere of influence like so many other Eastern European states were uninviting prospects. It was against this background that the Åland parliament expressed a wish for future reunion with Sweden. This, however, was immediately rejected by the Swedes.[14]

But there are a number of factors which have worked in favour of the present autonomy. There is really only one community in the Åland Islands, in contrast to many other areas of disputed minority territory elsewhere in Europe. Furthermore the Islands have no strategic significance – not only are they demilitarized, but even if they were not, it is doubtful if they would have a useful role to play in today's Europe. Nor, at the time of writing, do they have any economic significance.

Were these factors to change, and the Finnish government consequently wished or saw themselves obliged to increase the national presence there, then the present tranquillity in the Province, and its autonomy, would be more thoroughly tested.

Footnotes

1   Stephens, M., *Linguistic Minorities in Western Europe*, Llandysul Gomer Press, 1976, pp.270-274.
2   Stephens, *ibid.*, p.275.
3   *Statistical Yearbook of Finland, 1990*, published by the Central Statistical Office of Finland, Helsinki.
4   .Information from the Central Statistical Office of Finland.
5   Stephens, *op.cit.*, p.279.
6   Straka, M., *Handbuch der Europäischen Volksgruppen*, Vienna, Bramüller, 1970, p.257.
7   Stephens, *op.cit.*, pp.283-4.
8   Straka, *op.cit.*, p.252.
9   Modeen, T., 'The International Protection of the National Identity of the Åland Islands', in *Scandinavian Studies in Law*, 1973, p.179.
10 *Ibid.*
11 *Ibid.*, p.200.
12 In particular the USSR objected to the attempt to insert in the new act the possibility of obtaining an international guarantee in so far as the provisions for the protection of the Islanders nationality were concerned to replace the defunct League of Nations. Such a guarantee was considered to be a limitation of the Russian state's controlling power over Finland at the time. In the end the revised Act contained no guarantee but the Finnish government informed the Swedish government that it did not consider thereby its international obligations to be in any way affected. *Ibid.*, pp.188.93.
13 Details of the Act in *The Autonomy Act for Åland*, Mariehamn, Ålands Tidnings – Tryckeriat, 1978.
14 Modeen, *op.cit.*, p.189.

CONSTITUTION ACT OF FINLAND, 1919

ARTICLE 14

Finnish and Swedish shall be the national languages of the Republic. The right of Finnish citizens to use their mother tongue, whether Finnish or Swedish, before the courts and the administrative authorities, and to obtain from them documents in these languages, shall be guaranteed by law; care shall be taken that the rights of the Finnish speaking population and the rights of the Swedish speaking population of the country shall be promoted by the State upon an identical basis. The State shall provide for the intellectual and economic needs of the Finnish speaking and the Swedish speaking populations upon a similar basis.

ARTICLE 22

Laws and decrees as well as bills submitted by the Government to Parliament and the replies, recommendations, and other documents addressed by Parliament to the Government shall be drawn up in the Finnish and the Swedish languages.

ARTICLE 75

Every Finnish citizen must take part in, or make his contribution to, the defence of the Country as prescribed by law.

Every conscript,unless he otherwise desires, shall if possible be enrolled in a military unit of which the rank and file speak his own mother tongue (Finnish or Swedish) and shall receive his training in that language. Finnish shall be the language of command of the Armed Forces.

PARLIAMENT ACT, 1928

'In the transaction of business in Parliament, the Finnish or Swedish language shall be used.

The opinions and reports of committees as well as the written proposals of the Speaker's Conference and of the Committee for the Secretariat should be drawn up in these two languages.

Written communications addressed by the Government to Parliament should likewise be drawn up in Finnish and Swedish.'

DENMARK AND GERMANY – the German minority in Denmark and the Danish minority in Germany

by Klaus Carsten Pedersen

Name: Kongeriget Danmark
Constitutional status: parliamentary democracy, constitutional monarchy
International organizations: UN, EC, CE, CSCE
Political/military alliances: NATO
Population: 5,130,000
Minorities: Germans (in Jutland), Faroe Islanders (in Faroe Islands), Greenlanders/Inuit (in Greenland), 'new minorities' (mainly in Copenhagen)
Languages: Danish
Religion: Lutheran Protestant

Name: Bundesrepublik Deutschland
Constitutional status: Federal republic, divided into self-governing Lander
International organizations: UN, EC, CE, CSCE
Political/military alliances: NATO
Population: 78,090,000
Minorities: Danes (in Jutland), Sorbs (in Saxony), Frisians (North in Jutland and East in Emden), 'new minorities' (approximately 6 million in total, including children and other dependents of migrant workers, mainly Turks/Kurds (30%), Yugoslavs (15%), Italians (14%), Greeks (7%))
Languages: German
Religion: mainly Catholic and Lutheran Protestant

The Danish-German question arose in the borderland at the narrow base of the Jutland peninsula where the two peoples had met and mixed for more than a thousand years. Today the respective minority populations in each country are the subjects of parallel declarations from the two states which ensures that their minority rights will be respected.

The historical background

From pre-historic times Danes have inhabited the Jutland peninsula down to its narrowest and most easily defended part between the Slien fiord in the east and the Trene marshes in the west. Here, in the early 8th Century, the Danish king built a 15 km. long rampart which evolved over five centuries into a brick wall called *Dannevirke*. South of Dannevirke there was a thinly populated area to the river Eider, and to its south there was Holstein, inhabited by Saxons in the west who eventually overran and Germanized the Slavonic Wends in the east.

During the medieval period, the Holstein nobility gradually fought, bought and married their way into possession of estates and power north of Dannevirke in South Jutland which became the duchy of Slesvig (Schleswig in German) and they came to regard Slesvig as belonging to Holstein. However, in 1460 they elected the king of Denmark as their sovereign on the condition that the German Holstein and the Danish Slesvig were never in the future to be separated – thus creating both a real union between the duchies of Holstein and Slesvig and a personal union between these two duchies and the kingdom of Denmark. This state of affairs was to endure for 400 years.

In the early 19th Century, the growth in Europe of political and national awareness also affected relations between Danes and Germans. In somewhat simplified terms, the leaders in the purely German Holstein and the partly Germanized Slesvig wanted more autonomy from Denmark while Danes in Slesvig wanted to roll back the German-language domination in schools, church and administration in those parts of Slesvig where the language of the common people was still Danish.

The central question was where to draw the border between Denmark and Germany. A war in 1848-50 did not change the situation, but a growing number of Danes now wanted lose Holstein, keep Slesvig and thus reinstate the thousand-year old national border at Dannevirke or the river Eider. But Holstein would not leave without Slesvig.

In a brief but bloody war in 1864, Prussia came to the aid of the Germans in Holstein and parts of Slesvig, defeated Denmark and drew the border north of Slesvig, separating both duchies from Denmark. They did not gain independence, however, but were incorporated into the kingdom of Prussia and four years later into the new German Empire.

The shifting of the border meant that the minorities question changed radically. Before 1864, a large, fairly influential and fairly privileged German minority lived under the Danish crown – after 1864, a much smaller and increasingly underprivileged Danish minority found itself living in Germany. Tens of thousands emigrated to Denmark or overseas to avoid military service under the German flag and the forced Germanification of the education system, but more stayed on in order to keep their family farms and nurtured the hope of eventual reunification with Denmark.

During World War I, some 30,000 Danes in Slesvig were forced to fight on the German side, and with 6000 killed, the Danish minority losses were heavier than the German average. But the increasingly tough German treatment of the minority had been counter-productive and North Slesvig was probably more Danish in 1914 than it had been in 1864.

The border settlement

As a consequence of the defeat of Germany in 1918, a border revision was suddenly within reach. The question was how and how much, and Denmark took a difficult decision. Though many strongly demanded a restoration of the historic Dannevirke border, most Danes in Denmark and most leaders of the Danish minority in Slesvig chose to be guided not by historic right but by the will of the people now living in Slesvig. This view was built into the Versailles Peace Treaty of 1919.

Two plebiscites were held in 1920. In North Slesvig 74% voted for Denmark, and in a smaller middle zone, which included the large town of Flensborg, 80% voted for Germany. In the southern part of Slesvig there was no voting, since a massive German majority was a foregone conclusion. Between them, North and Middle Slesvig actually had a Danish majority of 53%, 88,000 votes for Denmark against 77,000 for Germany, but the new border of 1920 was drawn between the two zones, leaving minorities of 25,000 German voters in Denmark and 13,000 Danish voters in Germany.

There were both idealistic and practical motives behind Denmark's relative moderation and fairness. On the one hand, the belief in a population's right of self-determination had become firmly established in Denmark. On the other hand, Denmark was not eager to acquire an unmanageably large German minority with the repossession of former Danish territory, nor was Denmark eager to antagonize a Germany which, although defeated, would probably, by virtue of its size and industrial might, again become a powerful country.

The border settlement, fair though it was, did not satisfy everyone, being the subject of much debate and hope for revision on both sides. The Danish policy of moderation was put to its hardest test after Germany's second defeat in 1945. In the chaos and deprivation which followed the German surrender and burdened by hundreds of thousands of refugees from the east, many South Slesvigers had second thoughts about their Germanness and rediscovered their Danish roots and the attractions of Danish (and Nordic) economic, social and political structures. In the 1947 elections to the Schleswig-Holstein parliament in Kiel, Danish candidates received 100,000 votes, or a little over half the total number of votes cast in South Slesvig.

In view of the radically changed situation, Danish public opinion was now strongly in favour of a special status for South Slesvig, leaving open the possibility of a border revision if the new Danish majority there proved durable. It is not entirely clear whether the UK, the occupying power of northern Germany, would have backed such an arrangement had it been proposed by the Danish government. As it turned out, the Danish government and all political parties, with one exception, supported the policy of the permanent border.

It could be argued that by maintaining the border despite the new Danish majority south of it, Denmark betrayed the principle of self-determination. But in the first place, there were some doubts as to the sincerity of the swing in favour of Denmark, and secondly, there were the refugees from the eastern parts of the former German Reich. Either they would have to be expelled from Schleswig and accommodated elsewhere in Germany – and as their numbers rose everywhere, expulsion soon became unthinkable – or they would stay in Schleswig increasing its German population and turning the new Danish majority into a minority again. The latter is what happened, so leaving the border where it was did not, in the end, violate the principle of self-determination.

The less idealistic and more practical reasons for Danish restraint in the border question – not to incorporate a very large German minority in Denmark and not to antagonize Germany – were no less valid in 1945-47 than they had been in 1918-20. The border question was closed. What remained was the question of the rights of the national minorities north and south of the border.

The Danish minority in Germany had been squeezed ever since it was created by the German conquest in 1864. The German long-term aim was to consolidate the acquisition of Slesvig by rooting out Danish language, culture and political activity. Danes were also gradually uprooted from the land because many young men emigrated to avoid German military service and the pledge of allegiance to the Kaiser. Well over one-third of the population of North Slesvig emigrated between 1864 and 1914.

After 1920, the situation improved somewhat, but it deteriorated again with the growth of Nazism after 1933. After 1945, the Germans in what was to become the Land of Slesvig-Holstein felt threatened by the surge of pro-Danish sentiment, and they did what they could to contain it. The situation was confrontational.

The German minority in Denmark created by the border revision in 1920 was afforded much better conditions. The Danish policy had been made clear already at the peace conference in Paris in 1919: 'The reunification of the Danish

part of Slesvig with the Kingdom must ensure that all future citizens of the Danish state are treated according to the same liberal and democratic ground rules and enjoy the same rights.'

Danish laws, and the school laws in particular, gave the minority ample room for activity and consolidation. Very quickly the German minority had a flourishing school system based on German-language municipal schools and, increasingly, private schools enjoying generous state support under the uniquely liberal Danish Free School Act. Political activity was unhindered, and the German minority elected a representative to the Danish parliament.

It should also be noted that German civil servants in Denmark were spared the dilemma of their Danish opposite numbers in Germany of whether or not to take an oath of loyalty to the state, as oath-taking is not a Danish practice, either in civil or in military service. Danish civil servants and clergymen who did not take the German oath after 1864 were fired without pension.

World War II and its aftermath

However, the liberal atmosphere north of the border was totally disturbed by the German occupation of Denmark during the years 1940-45. The German minority had collaborated openly with the occupation forces and the Danish reaction in 1945 was harsh compared with normal Danish tradition and practice – though not compared with the backlash elsewhere in Europe.

Three thousand members of the German minority were interned and convicted, mostly on the basis of retroactive legislation. Although no one received the death sentence, many regarded the treatment as deeply unjust. German minority schools were also hard hit. Both the municipal and the private schools were closed and the premises of the latter confiscated, but private schools were reopened in 1946 with the same generous state support as Danish private schools, though for a period under strict supervision. Thus in Denmark, as in Germany, the situation was confrontational.

How did Denmark and Germany manage to pull themselves out of that confrontation? Generally speaking, Danish law and Danish political institutions provided a sufficient framework for the re-establishment of normal cultural, political and economic activities of the German minority. The main problem lay south of the border where new institutions had to be created, though with few democratic traditions to build on. The coincidence in 1949 of Social Democratic governments in both Copenhagen and Kiel and a Labour government in London facilitated communications, and the perceived threat from the USSR after the communist coup in Prague in 1948, were all factors leading to a better Danish-German understanding.

The Kiel Declaration

In September 1949, after negotiations with the Danish minority, the government of Schleswig-Holstein issued the so-called Kiel Declaration on the position of the minority. It assured the Danes (and Frisians) of South Slesvig of the ordinary democratic rights and civil liberties and non-discrimination. It specifically stated: 'Adherence to the Danish national community and Danish culture is free. It may neither be disputed nor [be] tested by the authorities.'

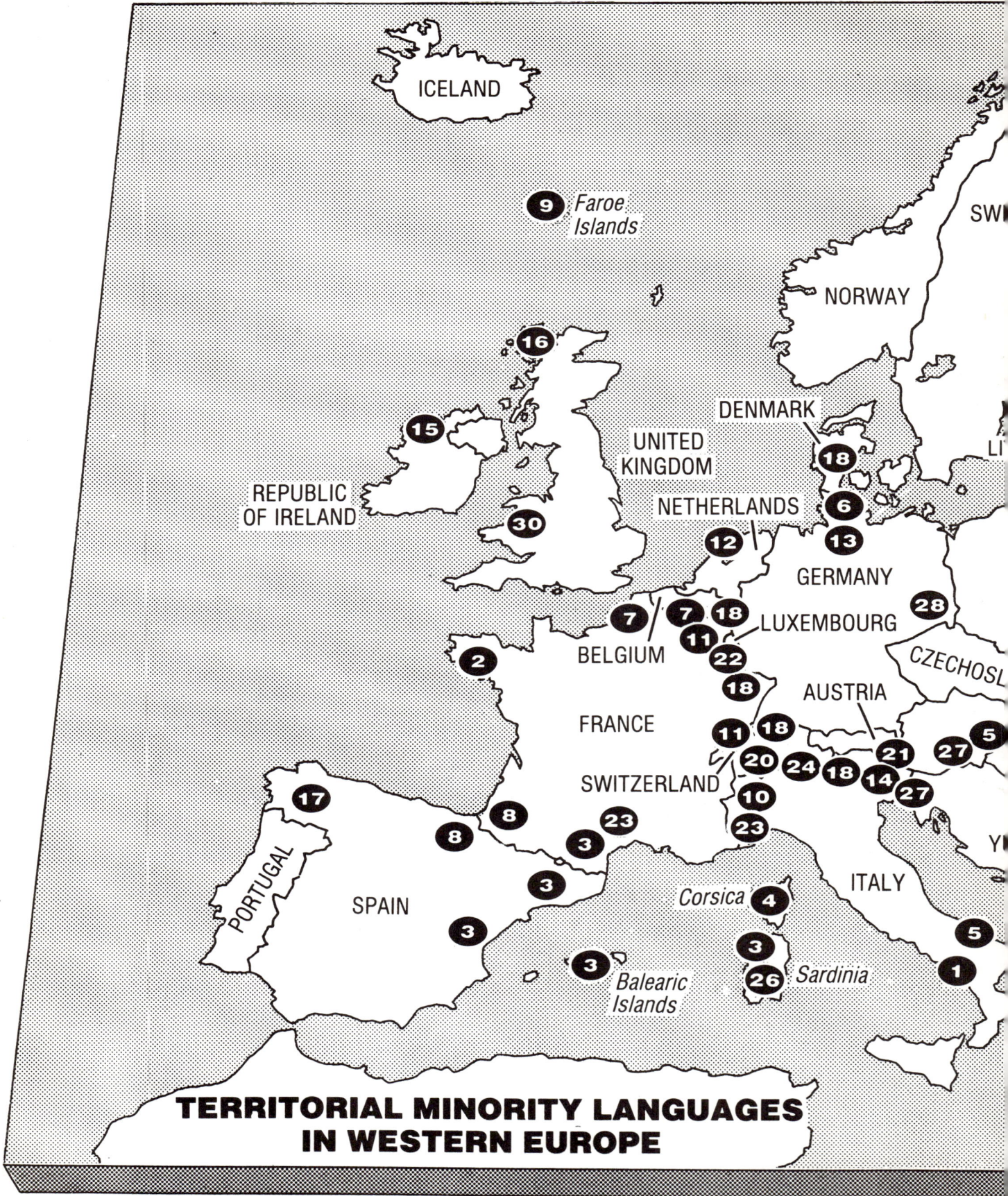

ICELAND

9 *Faroe Islands*

NORWAY

16

15

DENMARK

UNITED KINGDOM

18

REPUBLIC OF IRELAND

NETHERLANDS

6

30

12

13

GERMANY

28

7 **7** **18** LUXEMBOURG

11

22

CZECHOSL

2

BELGIUM

18

AUSTRIA

FRANCE

11 **18**

21 **27** **5**

20 **24** **18** **14**

17

SWITZERLAND

10

27

8

23

8

3 **23**

Y

PORTUGAL

3

ITALY

SPAIN

3

Corsica **4**

3

3

5

3 *Balearic Islands*

3

26 *Sardinia*

1

TERRITORIAL MINORITY LANGUAGES
IN WESTERN EUROPE

1. **Albanian** (Italy).

2. **Breton** (France).

3. **Catalan** (France, Italy-Sardinia, Spain-Catalunya, Valencia, Balearic Islands). State/regional language-(Spain).

4. **Corsican** (France)

5. **Croatian** (Austria, Italy). Schools/administrative language-(Austria).

6. **Danish** (Germany). Schools/administrative.

7. **Dutch/Flemish** (Belgium, France). State language-(Belgium).

8. **Euskara/Basque** (France, Spain). State/regional language-(Spain).

9. **Foroyskt/Faronese** (Denmark-Faroe Islands). Regional language.

10. **Franco-Provencal** (Italy-Piedmont and Foggia).

11. **French** (Belgium, Italy, Switzerland). State language-(Belgium and Switzerland).

12. **Frisian-West** (Netherlands). Regional language.

13. **Frisian-North** (Germany). Schools.

14. **Friulan** (Italy). Schools/administrative.

15. **Gaelic-Irish** (Republic of Ireland, UK-Northern Ireland). State language-(Republic of Ireland).

16. **Gaelic-Scots.** (UK-Scotland). Schools/administrative.

17. **Galician /Gallego** (Spain).

18. **German** (Belgium-Liege, Denmark-Slesvig, France-Alsace Lorraine, Italy-South Tyrol, Switzerland). State/regional language-(Belgium, Switzerland). Schools/administrative-(Denmark, Italy).

19. **Greek** (Italy).

20. **Italian** (Switzerland). State/regional language.

21. **Ladin** (Italy).

22. **Letzeburgesh** (Luxembourg). State language.

23. **Occitan** (France, Italy-Piedmont).

24. **Romanche/Romantsch** (Switzerland). State/regional language.

25. **Sami/Saami/Same** (Finland, Norway, Sweden). Schools.

26. **Sard** (Italy-Sardinia).

27. **Slovenian** (Austria, Italy). Schools/administrative.

28. **Sorb** (German). Schools/administrative.

29. **Swedish** (Finland). State language.

30. **Welsh** (UK-Wales). Regional language.

This chart is not comprehensive, nor does it include non-territorial minorities including 'new minorities' (migrant workers, refugees etc.) or travelling peoples (Romani gypsies). September 1991

This finally established in Germany the principle of free national and cultural choice, and inasmuch as the right of choice was personal, it was also a democratic breakthrough. It should be noted that this principle is not identical with the principle of self-determination, but relating as it does even to minorities behind firmly established borders, it is a very important supplement to the principle of self-determination.

The good intentions of the Kiel Declaration were not carried out in local practice however. Various forms of discrimination and harassment of the Danish minority continued, and matters came to a head when in 1954-58 a combination of gerrymandering and a 5% exclusion clause prevented Danish representation in the parliament of Schleswig-Holstein.

Denmark raised the problem in connection with meetings in NATO on the admission of the Federal Republic of Germany (West Germany) to the Western defence alliance. This brought the German federal government in Bonn into the picture and the result was two parallel, unilateral government declarations, the Bonn-Copenhagen Declarations of March 1955, on the positions of the minorities north and south of the border. The Danish minority was secured parliamentary representation in Kiel and the German minority schools in Denmark were granted the same examination rights as Danish schools.

The solution of the two declarations was chosen because Denmark opposed a bilateral treaty giving a large and powerful neighbour a right of oversight (however limited) into the internal affairs of a small, democratic country.

The main result of the Bonn-Copenhagen Declaration probably was confidence building and the paving of the way for the trust and goodwill which, supported by the authorities and public opinion, are the main basis on which a national minority may build a good existence. On both sides of the border the minority began to be viewed not as a threat but as an energetic and inspiring asset to the society and state in which it lives.

The present situation

After the turbulence of the post-war years, the minorities both north and south of the border seem to have stabilized in size: probably 15,000 to 20,000 (or 6% to 8%) in North Slesvig identify themselves as German and probably 50,000 to 60,000 (or 8% to 10%) in South Slesvig (Schleswig) feel Danish. Both communities tend to send their children to minority schools, but many fewer vote for specifically minority candidates.

The relaxation of tension has permitted the 'normal' political issues to play an increasing role in minority life so that in politics as well as in economic activities there are assimilation processes at work in the border region. And with Danish-German partnership in NATO followed by partnership in the EC, the significance of the state border is now rapidly diminishing.

However, a peaceful competition between Danish and German culture and between Danish and German solutions to common problems seems bound to continue alongside with, and as a productive supplement to, peaceful cooperation and integration.

Some lessons

Some of the main factors behind the present situation seem to be a democratic political culture leading to respect for civil rights, including the right of self-determination and the right of free national and cultural choice; moderation with regard to claims based on historic rights to specific pieces of land; constructive unilateral steps; focus on areas of common or mutual interest; and, at crucial times, an outside catalyst.

Furthermore it demonstrates that the respective size neither of the minority nor of the state concerned should be in a factor in determining the provision of minority rights. Although unified Germany is 20 times larger than Denmark, the guarantees and treatment remain the essentially the same in both states. During the crucial time of decision, the immediate post-war period, great power influence upon a defeated and divided, but rapidly democratizing, Germany proved decisive in ensuring a political solution to an ethnic and territorial problem.

The Danish-German minority situation is by definition unique and so may be the solution, but parts of it may be relevant to other cases. Its attraction is that it worked.

COPENHAGEN DECLARATION, 1955

Desiring to promote peaceful living together among the population on either side of the Danish-German frontier and thereby also to promote the general development of friendly relations between the Kingdom of Denmark and the Federal Republic of Germany, and

Referring to article 14 of the European Convention on Human Rights according to which all rights and freedoms set forth in the Convention shall be secured to everybody without discrimination on the ground of association with a national minority,

The Royal Danish Government, in confirmation of the legal principles already applying to the German minority in North Slesvig – as also expressed in the declaration made by the then Danish Prime Minister Hans Hedtoft on 27 October 1949 to representatives of that minority (the so-called Cophenhagen Note)

DECLARES AS FOLLOWS:

Under Danish law – the Constitution of the Kingdom of Denmark of 5 June 1953, and supplementary legislation – every citizen, and consequently everybody belonging to the German minority, irrespective of his language, enjoys the following rights and freedoms:

1. Inviolability of personal liberty;

2. Equality before the law;

3. Freedom of creed and conscience;

4. Freedom of expression and of the press;

5. Freedom of assembly and association;

6. The right freely to choose occupation and place of work;

7. Inviolability of the dwelling;

8. The right freely to form political parties;

9. Equal access for everybody to public employment according to merits, suitability and professional qualifications, which implies that in matters relating to civil servants, employees, and workers in public service no distinction must be made between persons belonging to the German minority and other citizens;

10. General, direct, equal, free and secret franchise, applying also in municipal elections;

11. The right of anybody who believes that his rights have been violated by the authorities to invoke the protection of the courts of law;

12. The right to equal treatment, which means that nobody may suffer prejudice or be favoured because of his descent, language origin or political opinion.

In consequence of these principles of law, it is hereby established as follows:

1. Profession of German nationality and German culture is free and must not be challenged or examined by the authorities.

2. Persons belonging to the German minority and their organizations may not be prevented from using, orally or in writing, the language which they prefer. Use of the German language before the tribunals and administrative authorities is subject to the legislative provisions on the matter.

3. In virtue of the principle of freedom of education which applies in Denmark, schools for general education, folk high-schools (including vocational) and kindergardens may be established by the German minority pursuant to law.

4. When the legislation on local government makes the method of proportional representation applicable to the appointment of committees of municipal councils, representatives of the German minority take part in the work of committees in proportion to their numbers.

5. The Danish Government recommends that, within the framework of the rules which may at any time apply to the use of the state broadcasting system, reasonable regard shall be paid to the German minority.

6. With respect to subventions and other grants from public funds which are allocated at discretion, no distinction will be made between persons belonging to the German minority and other citizens.

7. When public notices are made, reasonable regard shall be paid to the daily press of the German minority.

8. The special interest of the German minority in cultivating their religious, cultural and professional relations with Germany is recognized.

BELGIUM

by Professor Marc J. Bossuyt and Dick Leonard[1]

Name: Royaume de Belgique/Koninkrijk van Belgie
Constitutional status: parliamentary democracy, constitutional monarchy, federated state (see below)
International organizations: UN, EC, CE, CSCE
Political/military alliances: NATO
Population: 9,880,000
Minorities: Flemings, Walloons, Germans, 'New minorities' (about 7% – Italian, Spanish, Moroccan, Turkish, African)
Languages: Flemish/Dutch (57%), French (42%), German (1%)
Religion: Catholic

The historic background

Belgium became an independent state in 1830 after a successful uprising against the Dutch king, who had been the sovereign of the reunited Netherlands since 1815. As had been the case for centuries, the population of southern Belgium (the Walloon area) spoke French dialects, while the population of northern Belgium (Flanders) spoke Dutch dialects. However the ruling classes in Flanders were French-speaking, the result of a long-drawn-out process which was aided by a deliberate policy of 'Francization', particularly after the Belgian independence.

In social life the Francization policy was revealed in the fact that any Flemish-speaking Fleming who succeeded in climbing the social ladder was obliged to become 'francized' if he wished to be received in 'good' society. A Fleming who refused to meet this requirement would have been virtually ostracized. In official life in every field – military, administrative, legal and educational – all matters above a certain level were dealt with in French, including throughout Flanders.

Gradually however, this policy was amended. The first linguistic law of 1873 introduced the use of Dutch in criminal proceedings in Flanders; a law of 1898 provided for the publication of future Acts of Parliament in French and Dutch. Nevertheless, up to 1930, there was no Dutch-language university in Belgium.

The result of this policy was that around 1930 the linguistic situation in Belgium was roughly as follows. The aristocracy spoke French and did not know either Dutch or the Flemish dialect. The same was true in general of people of social standing in the towns, except that they tended to have a rudimentary knowledge of Dutch/Flemish. In the towns, but more particularly in the countryside, there was a middle class that normally spoke Flemish dialect but spoke and wrote French whenever they wished to show signs of distinction.

Thus the situation in Flanders was that, with a few rare exceptions, the population was not fluent in the literary language (Dutch) which corresponded to the language of the people (Flemish). Between 1830 and 1914 there had been a reaction from certain Flemish literary figures, who had only a limited influence on the upper middle class but who received more support from the lower middleclass. This reaction was accompanied by a certain bitterness against the disdain shown to the Flemish language of the people.

The switch after the 1914-18 war from an electoral system based on qualification by tax assessment to straightforward universal male suffrage in 1920[2] brought a far-reaching change in the social climate. There was a linguistic revolt of the Flemish people against its ruling class, which took the form of a Flemish national feeling that was sometimes violently anti-Belgian. Yet it was the electoral reform which was the necessary and, in the end, sufficient condition for them to win parity for their language. In the previous, unreformed, parliament not a single speech in Dutch had been made until 1889, over 50 years after its foundation. Even so, it took another 40 or so years before the full effect of the Dutch-speaking majority made itself felt.

The linguistic laws of the 1930s

By 1930 most Belgian politicians agreed that there was a need for far-reaching linguistic reform. A whole body of legislation, aimed at placing the two languages of French and Dutch on an equal footing, was agreed upon and implemented. As the introduction of a bilingual system on both sides of the language border was not accepted, the principle of equality was implemented by introducing a unilingual Dutch system in Flanders, and French unilingualism in the Walloon area.

An Act of 1932 on the use of languages in primary and secondary education provided that in Flanders as well as in the Walloon area the language used in official education would be that of the region. Private education could be subsidized and have its certificates recognized only if it, too, were given in the language of the region. As a result the Flemings got a new elite which remained Flemish even when they occupied high social positions.

However, the process of Francization continued along the language boundary, in Brussels and in the Flemish communes on its outskirts. Because of the social predominance of the French language (and, in the case of communes on the outskirts of Brussels, a migration of French-speaking inhabitants of Brussels to those communes) Francization affected not only Flemings who had risen in the social scale, but also the lower middle class and sometimes also the working class.

The 1932 legislation allowed communes on the language boundary to make educational and administrative adjustments on the basis of 10-yearly censuses including questions on language. The result of the census in 1947 showed how Francization had developed. As the effect of the adjustments was almost entirely one way – in favour of the French-speaking community – the Flemish claimed integrity for their territory, as a corollary of the existence of Flemish national feeling. The census of 1947 resulted in a serious clash between the two linguistic communities: the Walloons charged the Flemings with demographic imperialism while the Flemings accused the Walloons of geographical imperialism.

The linguistic laws of the 1960s

Instead of holding a new language census around 1960, the great majority of Belgian politicians agreed to fix the language boundary once and for all. An Act of 8 November 1962 established the language boundary on the general basis of the report of the 'Centre Harmel', which was set up in 1948 to study linguistic problems.

An Act of 30 July 1963 once again stipulated that official education should be given in the language of the region and that private education, if it was to receive grants and have its own certificates recognized, must also be given in that language. An Act of 2 August 1963 deals with the position of

certain Flemish communes on the outskirts of Brussels, allowing certain exceptions in primary education for the benefit of the French-speaking inhabitants of those communes.[3]

The constitutional reform of the 1970s

In 1970 the Belgian state structure underwent major changes through a revision of its constitution introducing 'cultural autonomy' for its Dutch-speaking and French-speaking communities. More and more the Flemish and Walloon communities became conscious of their own identity and perceived their interests differently. The constitutional revision of 1970 provided for:

a) the division into Dutch- and French-speaking groups of all members of the national parliament, for them to exercise as members of two cultural councils legislative authority in cultural matters over the citizens belonging to their respective cultural community (new article 32 *bis* of the constitution);

b) the division of Belgium into four linguistic territories:)the unilingual Dutch, French, and German territories and the bilingual territory of Brussels-Capital (new article 3 *bis* of the constitution). No change in the borders of the four territories is possible except by a law adopted by a majority of each of the two linguistic groups, the majority of each group being present, and a two-thirds majority of all members of the chamber of the parliament participating in the vote;

c) the division of Belgium into three regions: a Flemish region, a Walloon region and a Brussels region (article 107 *quater* of the constitution); the composition and competence of the regional organs to be determined by laws adopted by specially qualified majorities;

d) the institution of an 'alarm bell' procedure whereby three-quarters of the members of any linguistic group in the parliament may declare that the provisions of a draft law which may endanger the relations between the communities shall be referred to the Council of Ministers;

e) parity between Dutch- and French-speaking Ministers, with the exception of the Prime Minister (new article 86 *bis* is of the constitution).

The constitutional reform of the 1980s

A persistent call for greater autonomy led to another revision of the constitution in 1980, which put into effect the most profound institutional reform in Belgian history. Henceforth at the federal level there are three communities (Flemish-, French- and German-speaking) and three regions (Flemish, Walloon and Brussels). The subjects of the communities are determined *ratione personae*, the subjects of the regions are determined *ratione loci*. While Flanders comprises both the Flemish community and the Flemish region, Wallonia only consists of the Walloon region, greatly overlapping the French community *ratione loci*, but *ratione materiae* distinct from it.

Pending a more definite solution for Brussels-Capital, the executive for the Brussels regions operates within the national government. The administrative region of Brussels-Capital is composed of the City of Brussels and 18 neighbouring municipalities.

Brussels-Capital did not originally have its own legislative body. As far as the 'communal' matters are concerned, the Flemish community norms apply to the Dutch-speaking institutions, the French community norms to the French-speaking institutions and the national laws to the bi-communal institutions and to the persons on the territory of Brussels-Capital. The national laws apply to regional matters. For those matters which are localized in the territory of Brussels-Capital, a Ministerial Committee composed of one minister and two secretaries of state belonging to the national Cabinet are responsible. They act by consensus; in the absence of consensus the matter is deferred to the full Cabinet.

The Flemish community and the Flemish region have one common executive and legislature, which functions independently from the national government and legislature in community as well as regional powers. The Walloon region and the French community each have a distinct executive and legislature, also independent from the national government and respectively competent for regional and community matters. The community powers concern the so-called 'matters linked to the person' and includes social affairs, health and welfare, in addition to cultural affairs. The regional powers range from environmental protection, physical planning, housing and inland waterways to regional economic policy, energy policy, employment and research.

The question remains whether the plan of central laws and regional and communal decrees is a correct decision, or whether a more far-reaching transfer of authority to the regions should not be accompanied by accepting the principle of the priority of national norms under strict conditions. The present system provides only for the settlement of conflicts of jurisdiction by a new Court of Arbitration, which started work in 1985 and which is composed of six Dutch-speaking and six French-speaking members, half of them lawyers and half former politicians. It is invested with the power of judicial review of legislation on the basis of the power conferring provisions in, and some fundamental rights protected by, the constitution.

The current financial arrangement for the communities and the regions is the weak point of the reform. The component member units receive appropriations from the national budget and have only limited taxation powers of their own. However, it is generally felt that, in order to be able to implement their own policies in their own areas of jurisdiction, the communities and regions should have their own financial resources and should bear full financial responsibility for their own policies.

The 1980 state reform was not satisfactory because a definitive settlement for the Brussels region was omitted. The specific problems in Brussels concern the delimitation of its territory and the protection of the Flemish minority.

It was not until the 1988 constitutional amendments that the Brussels-Capital Region got its own legislative and executive bodies, having the same competence as its Flemish and Walloon counterparts. The parity between the Dutch- and French-speaking members of the executive, the president excluded, is guaranteed. The executive acts by consensus.

In the Brussels region, which belongs to both the Flemish and French community, the French and Flemish community laws apply respectively to the French- and Dutch-speaking institutions.

The community legislations can delegate the exercise of their powers in the Brussels region to the Flemish and French community commissions. These commissions are composed of the respective Flemish and French members of the Brussels legislature. They can legislate in a joint session upon 'bi-communitarian institutions' (those institutions in Brussels which belong neither to the French nor Flemish community).

Another shortcoming of the 1980 state reform is the 'double mandate'. With the exception of the German community and Brussels-Capital legislatures, for which separate elections are held, all other legislatures are composed of members of the national bicameral parliament who are elected in the corresponding region or community. Thus, the independence of the regions and communities from the national level of government is not yet effective.

Future constitutional amendments are expected to change the composition of the legislatures. Members of the (national) House of Representatives will be excluded from membership of the regional and community legislatures. The (national) Senate could be composed of the members of these legislatures in order to guarantee the representation of the regions at the national legislative level. The powers of the Senate are likely to be limited.

In practice the actual state structure is somewhat confused due to a lack of clarity in the terms of the law and the incomplete character of the reform. No homogenous policy-packages have been transferred to the communities or regions and the limits between the several fields of jurisdiction are far from clear-cut. Unlike other federally organized states, the national norms do not prevail over the regional or community norms. Co-operation between the different levels of government is therefore indispensable for the distribution of powers to operate.

The financial arrangements are governed by the principles of financial responsibility of the regions and communities and solidarity between the federal and federated entities. The latter receive appropriations from the national budget (amounting to 40% of the national budget). Their own taxation powers are limited. In order to maintain an equal level of welfare throughout the country, less prosperous regions (ie. Wallonia) may receive additional national financial support.

Notwithstanding the increase in regional autonomy in 1989, the national legislature still decides basically which financial means will be attributed to the member units. It is generally felt that in order to be able to implement their own policies in their own areas of jurisdiction, the communities and regions should have their own financial resources and should bear full financial responsibility for their own policies.

A further transfer of powers to the regions will probably take place in the near future. The residuary powers may be transferred from the national to the federated entities. The participation by the regions and communities in the negotiating and signing of international treaties may also be expanded.

Linguistic flashpoints remain, one of which is the tiny commune of the Fourons, which has a French-speaking majority but which is part of the Dutch-speaking province of Limburg. Crises over this commune have brought about the fall of three governments over 20 years, most recently in 1987. This led to a fresh round of constitutional reform, including the direct election of a regional Council for

Brussels, with built-in safeguards for the majority in the capital. Further powers were transferred at the same time to the Flemish and Walloon regions and to the language communities.

The sociological dimension

Historically, the language issue in Belgium took the form of a struggle by the Flemings for equality with the French-speaking Belgians who formed the governing elite. In the 1960s this was paralleled by a militant movement of French-speakers who asserted that the boot was now on the other foot: that it was the French language that was discriminated against. This claim did have some foundation, but – partly owing to the constitutional changes of recent years – neither side now appears to have a serious basis for complaint. What injustices remain are essentially of a marginal nature.

The 1963 language laws ostensibly promoted equality between the two language groups. Effectively, however, they put French speakers at a disadvantage. The French-speaking population of Brussels was most directly affected. Three provisions, in particular, hit them hard.

Firstly, jobs in the public service in Brussels were to be divided on a 50-50 basis, even though Brussels was four-fifths Francophone. Secondly, top civil-service jobs would be open only to recruits competent in both languages. As middle-class Flemings almost invariably spoke good French, while middle-class Walloons seldom bothered to master Dutch, this threatened to exclude the latter from the higher echelons of the government service.

The final major grievance concerned the freezing of the 'linguistic' boundary, which had previously been revised with each decennial census. This meant that French-speakers in the peripheral suburbs of Brussels would remain under Dutch-speaking administrations, even when they had become the majority.

It was not only political and constitutional changes which helped the Flemish cause. Economic changes, particularly since the World War II, have transformed Flanders from what the leading Flemish bank had described as 'an impoverished and backward agricultural area'. Since 1945 investment, particularly from abroad, has flowed into Flanders, attracted by its proximity to the sea and to major ports such as Antwerp, its surplus labour and low wages at a time of general labour scarcity and its better industrial climate, as measured by a substantially lower incidence of strikes. At the same time French-speaking Wallonia, burdened with its inheritance of old heavy industries, was entering into a long period of relative decline.

The consequence is that today Flanders is a shop-window for modern technology, while Wallonia is painfully struggling to catch up, with a higher unemployment rate, slower growth and much lower profit ratios. The 1980 devolution programme gave the Flemish regional executive effective control of the Flemish economy, while leaving the Walloon regional executive the same responsibilities in Wallonia.

The Flemings now have few, if any, remaining grounds for feeling any sense of inferiority. They are the majority, their part of the country is the more prosperous half and it is governed by Flemings in the Flemish interest. In the national government of Belgium their influence is predominant, despite mathematical formulae designed to give the French-speakers a 50% share. For example, 12 of the last 13 governments have been led by a Dutch-speaker, and one exception was a caretaker administration which lasted only a few months.

As for the French-speakers, the penalties inflicted by the 1963 language laws have been attenuated with time. Ambitious young Francophones now take their studies of Dutch seriously, and there are many cases of French-speaking parents deliberately enrolling their children in the Dutch-speaking schools of Brussels, or even of moving to neighbouring towns in Flanders, in order that they should grow up completely bilingual.

In the early 1970s the main political parties in Belgium (Christian-Democrats, Socialists and Liberals) split each on linguistic lines into two distinct parties. At the end of that decade three 'linguistic' parties participated in a government: the *Rassemblement wallon* in 1974-1977, and the *Front democratique des francophones* together with the *Volksunie* in 1977-1979.

The elections of the 1980s resulted in a continuous decline of the linguistic parties. Even at their height they together they had received only 22% of the total vote and had never held the primary political allegiance of the majority of the population. In particular, after the elections of 1985 the *Rassemblement wallon* disappeared, the *Front democratique des francophones* was considerably weakened, and the *Volksunie* also lost some seats. The latter became nevertheless part of the government coalition formed after the 1987 elections. In a period of economic crisis the electorate returned to the main political parties.

Linguistic flashpoints such as Fourons remain as localized (and publicized) grievances. The consequence has been that language disputes have disappeared from the top of the Belgian political agenda. If this state of affairs continues, a heavy burden will have been lifted from Belgian consciousness.

Some lessons

Some aspects of the Belgian political structure might usefully be transferred to other plural European societies. These include: the use of proportional representation in all elections; the requirement that a fixed proportion of ministers should come from each community; the devolution, both to geographical and community (in this case linguistic) authorities, of important economic, social and cultural powers; and institutional arrangements, such as the 'alarm bell' procedure and the Court of Arbitration for trying to avoid or resolve disputes between the communities.

What Belgium could most usefully lend elsewhere may not, unfortunately, be transferable. It is the spirit of compromise which seems deeply ingrained in the Belgian psyche. It is the result of not just of harbouring different communities, but of having to live with a succession of occupying powers – Bungundians, Spaniards, Austrians, French and Dutch – over five centuries. For most of this time Belgians were able to work out a modus vivendi with their occupiers, which enabled them to get on with their own lives in tolerable circumstances. With this history behind them, Belgians have generally found means of resolving their own disputes, or at least containing them until such time as passions have cooled.

Footnotes

[1] The article on Belgium was originally published in two parts with Prof. Bossuyt as the author of Part I, which dealt mainly with the constitutional arrangements and Dick Leonard as the author of Part II, on the language and sociology of present day Belgium. For this edition the two sections have been merged. Most, but not all, of the article from the beginning of the text to the end of the section on *The constitutional reforms in the 1980s* is the work of Prof. Bossuyt, and similarly most, but not all, of the text from the beginning of the section on *The sociological dimension* to the end of the text is by Dick Leonard.

[2] Women had to wait until 1948 before they were granted the vote.

[3] See also the European Court of Human Rights' judgement in the Belgian Linguistic cases of 27 July 1968. Also see *Belgium's Walloons and Flemings*, MRG Report, 1980.

BELGIUM CONSTITUTION, 1831,
REVISION OF 1980

ARTICLE 3 *bis*

Belgium comprises four linguistic regions: the French-language region, the Dutch-language region, the bilingual region of Brussels-Capital, and the German-language region.

3 trente

Belgium comprises three cultural communities: French, Dutch and German. Each community enjoys the powers vested in it by the Constitution, or such legislation as shall be enacted in virtue thereof.

ARTICLE 59 *bis*

There is to be a Cultural Council for the French cultural community, made up of the members of the French linguistic group of both Houses, and a Cultural Council for the Dutch cultural community, made up of the Dutch linguistic community.

59 trente

There is to be a Cultural Council for the German-speakers of the cantons de L'Est.

ARTICLE 107 *bis*

Belgium comprises three regions: the Walloon region, the Flemish region and the Brussels region...'

SWITZERLAND
by Dr. Jonathan Steinberg

Name: Schweizerische Eidgenossenschaft, Confédération Suisse, Confederazione Svizzera
Constitutional status: democratic confederation of largely self-governing cantons
International organizations: EFTA, CE, CSCE
Political/military alliances: neutral
Population: 6,723,000 (1983)
Population composition: German-speakers (65%); French-speakers (18%); Italian-speakers (10%); Romansch/Romanche-speakers (1%) of population; plus immigrants/guest-workers (15.47%) of population
Languages: German, French, Italian, Romansch/Romanche
Religion: Catholic, Protestant

When the author asked the Swiss Embassy in London for the text of their law or laws covering minority rights, he received a huffy reply from his friend there, a diplomat: 'We don't need minority protection; in Switzerland we are all members of minority groups.' This remark is a common one and it is quite true.

A nation of minorities

In Switzerland, there is no majority – no equivalent of white, English-speaking and Protestant Christians in the UK or the USA. It is true that the German-Swiss make up two-thirds of all Swiss citizens, but the language they speak, *Schwyzerdutsch*, turns them into a minority group within the German-speaking world and gives them many of the touchy attitudes to be found among Welsh or Catalan speakers. German-Swiss divide between Protestant and Catholic, between highland and lowland, between urban and rural, between large canton and small canton, between radical and conservative, so that even within the majority Germanic world most Swiss do indeed feel themselves 'members of a minority group'.

Switzerland as a state among states belongs to a tiny minority. One of the very few states in the world committed to international neutrality, it constitutes a minority of one in its attitude to international organizations. In a referendum in 1986 the Swiss voters turned down, as they had done on two previous occasions, a government decision to join the United Nations. In 1991, the Swiss government, although it had agreed to support sanctions against Iraq, refused to allow allied planes on their way to the Gulf to enter Swiss air space. Other neutral European states, Austria, Sweden and Finland, have not gone so far.

Switzerland is also in a minority in its extreme commitment to the democratic process. All legislation at either federal or cantonal level can be altered either by referendum or by initiative, that is, by formal procedures in which the citizen replaces the lawmaker. Issues such as the introduction of value-added tax, limitation on the number of foreign workers, adoption of summer time, footpath networks for hikers, revision of the law on atomic energy, legalization of induced abortion and consumer protection go almost automatically to the 'sovereign', as the 'people' are fondly called in Swiss political usage. The commitment to democracy extends to school curricula, to the language of instruction and to issues such as the local sewers.[1]

Switzerland may be the richest country in the world (depending on how the calculations are made), and certainly is so in terms of living standards for the majority, rather than of a small elite. It has more banks than dentists. It has almost no unemployment (in the first half of 1990 less than 0.5%), and almost no strikes. (Over the entire decade of 1980s there were almost 24 strikes; in 1987 there were none; 1988, four; 1989, two.). Its citizenry is fully armed, and all adult males serve first in the army and then in the reserve until the age of 50. As Machiavelli observed in the 16th Century, 'the Swiss are most armed and most free'. An army of some 750,000 can be mobilized within a few days of hostilities. Only Israel has a population so thoroughly militarized, and it uses the Swiss mobilization procedures.

These very peculiarities lead the Swiss to think that collectively they are a kind of national minority, *Sonderfall Schweiz*, the 'Swiss special case'. They see themselves as an embattled small people surrounded by a dangerous and hostile world, constantly threatened by alien powers and alien trends. The country has magnificent scenery but few natural resources. A Gulf War or Chernobyl between them can cause a catastrophe for the tourist industry – estimated to rank third among Swiss industries, after machines and textiles, but ahead of watches.

The Japanese threatened with their cheap digitals to ruin the watch industry; foreign states may put up trade barriers against which a tiny trading country has no redress; wild currency fluctuations caused by what the Swiss regard as irresponsible economic policies by the large states push the Swiss franc out of international competition. (In 1970 the pound sterling bought 10 Swiss francs, in 1991 less than 2.5; the dollar used to buy over 4 francs, today less than 1.5) Through no fault of their own, indeed, through their virtues, Swiss products become more and more expensive for foreigners.

There is in Switzerland a fortress mentality, which underlies the confidence and the success. The Swiss, not always consciously, feel that their wealth, their way of life, their independence, their neutrality are always at risk. Like the Jews and other minorities, below the conscious level, there is a feeling of precariousness which the Swiss respond to by hard work. Nowhere in Europe is the work ethic so entrenched, so pervasive and so powerful.

In the early 1980s Grenchen, the centre of the traditional watch industry, looked like becoming a ghost town. Today the Swatch has turned it into an eldorado again. Just as in the 1870s and 1880s, Switzerland fought back against the cheap American mass-produced Waltham watch, so in the 1980s by sheer hard work, flexibility, ruthlessness (complete managements forcibly retired), and ingenuity, they have beaten the Japanese at their own game, the only Western country to have done so.

None of this may look at first as if it ought to be discussed in a report devoted to minorities, but the collective background explains in part the characteristic reply offered by the diplomat. If a whole country feels itself to be a minority in the world, surely it does not need to worry about minority rights. In the author's opinion, in this the Swiss delude themselves, just conceivably rather dangerously.

It was Alexis de Tocqueville in his *Democracy in America*, written in the 1830s, who first noticed how intolerant genuine democracy can be. There was, he saw, in the New England townships a kind of 'tyranny of the majority' which suppressed unpopular or eccentric thought and deed. Nathaniel Hawthorne in his *The Scarlet Letter* and *The Blithedale Romance*, rang the changes on the theme, especially in the latter, less well-known novel, in which a utopian commune tries to create the perfect society and ends

by perfecting a special kind of tyranny.

Switzerland has the same democratic vices. Swiss communities are not tolerant nor easily amused. They distrust wit and frivolity. They want their governors to be as much like themselves as possible. They distrust dissent and have resisted longer and more bitterly the acceptance of conscientious objection than any other civilized society in the world. Article 18 of the Swiss Constitution states that 'Every Swiss is obliged to perform military service.' In June 1991, for the first time, the voters approved a tiny amendement to the constitution which 'decriminalized' conscientious objection. Not even membership of pacifist religious communities will exempt a man but, under certain circumstances, such persons may do their service in branches without weapons like the medical corps. The democracy will not tolerate exemptions.

The Swiss are not all that keen on the very variety which so strikes the observant foreigner. Catholics and Protestant cantons fought a civil war in 1847 and, while Bismarck contemptuously dismissed it as a 'rabbit shoot', it left a legacy of communal bitterness. A historian of the Catholic community has written of 'the Ghetto mentality' of Swiss Catholics.[2] Even among Swiss Catholics political hostilities run deep. Party rivalry in the Italian-speaking Canton of Ticino frequently erupted into physical violence in the 19th Century and on occasions even in the 20th Century. Swiss police were no more tolerant of hippy and counter-culture manifestations in the 1970s than the notorious German and French police forces.

Political structures

Swiss political structures cope with separatism better than they do with dissenting behaviour because Swiss politics crumbles so easily into smaller and sub-divisible units. Swiss cantons frequently have enclaves of other cantons within them or, as in the Canton Schaffhausen, bits of Germany. Along the shores of Lake Lugano, there is the Italian community of Campione d'Italia, completely surrounded by the Swiss Canton Ticino. The Swiss are not bothered by the fact that political entities have, so to speak, holes in them. They live comfortably with political maps that look like patchwork quilts.

This process was illustrated by the case of the Jurassiens, a minority group who behaved as if they were an oppressed national minority similar to many of the other regional or separatist movements of Europe. During the struggle for a 'Free Jura' of the 1960s and 1970s, the Jurassien separatists – French-speaking Roman Catholic inhabitants of what were then the north-western districts of Canton Bern – took up the techniques of liberation movements everywhere. 'Jura libre' signs covered the walls of public buildings in Porrentruy and Delémont; the odd bomb went off to underline the sentiments.

Since political units have to be, first, democratic and then built from the bottom, there was no difficulty in principle in subdividing Canton Bern to permit the Jurassiens to form their own Canton. It was self-evident that French-speaking Protestant villages dotted among the Catholic ones would stay with Bern, and in the case of Moutier the division might be made street by street.

The difficulty lay not in the principle but in the people. The voters of Bern took a decade and some violence before they agreed to sever the offending districts from the body politic. The new canton of Jura was admitted to the Swiss Federation on 1 January 1979. Divisible, democratic units make it possible for certain sorts of minority to be made comfortable within the larger framework.

Federalism helps too. In Switzerland the 3000 communes spend as much as the federal government. The 26 cantons each have considerable powers over the lives of their citizenry. Catholic cantons behave differently from Protestant ones but all have got used to the existence of pockets of minority culture within their boundaries. Cantons like Fribourg, Valais or Graubünden have learned to allow local communities cultural sovereignty right down to the village level. Language borders cross political borders, and it is only by the different flowers in the window boxes that one can tell that one has passed from, say, German to French Fribourg.

The language division

Language poses minority problems of its own. Switzerland recognizes four official languages – German, French, Italian and Romanche. The first three appear by law on state documents, national monuments, federal regulations and instructions, the railway timetables and by custom on a variety of labels, announcements, journals and advertisements. Announcers on planes and at railway stations employ the language most likely to be used. In parliament Italian-speaking deputies have the right to speak in Italian, and do so on ceremonial occasions in the full chamber. If they want to be understood, and always at committee stage, they speak German or French.

Swiss-German speakers break down into three distinct linguistic variants and countless local dialects. Swiss-German, when spoken in the more remote regions, sometimes baffles Swiss Germans themselves, and the whole linguistic thicket of dialect keeps the foreigners out.

French and Italian Swiss, irrespective of any other divisions among them, share a common sense that they belong to minority communities. The preponderance of German Switzerland is more than just weight of numbers. German Switzerland houses the big banks, the big companies and the big investors. French and Italian Swiss resent the economic hegemony of the German Swiss business community, a resentment felt underneath all the politeness that marks interlinguistic relations.

French Swiss rarely learn Swiss-German, preferring if they make the effort at all to learn proper German, what Swiss-Germans tend to call 'High German' or 'Written German', so that personal encounters across the Franco-Germanic linguistic borders normally take place in French. Swiss-Germans like to practise and Swiss-French cannot be bothered.[3] French Swiss look to Paris culturally and tend to regard dialect as 'patois', a sign of provinciality and backwardness. Nobody, save the Swiss Germans, bothers to learn Italian, and the grievance of the Italian Swiss about the dominance of Swiss Germans is as keenly felt as in French Switzerland.

Romanche speakers make up the most embattled and endangered linguistic minority. Whereas about 10% of the resident population of Switzerland speak Italian and just under 20% speak French, less than 1% still speak the ancient Romanche vernacular of the high mountains in the Grisons.

There are, according to the most recent linguistic census, now less than 50,000 Romanche speakers left. All the Romanche communities are contained within the tri-lingual Canton of Graubünden (or Grisons in French, or Grigioni in Italian, or Grischun in Romanche). During the past century more than 40 formerly Romanche-speaking communities have gone over to German and the proportion of the inhabitants of the Canton who use Romanche regularly has fallen from just under half to just under a quarter.

Economic realities, not persecution of minorities, account for the disappearance of Romanche. Like all economies of the European periphery, the high valley economies of Graubünden cannot compete with the lowlands. Either the population descends to the plain to work and hence the Romanche-speaking pool dribbles away down the slops of the Alps; or enterprise, stimulated by well-meaning governments, finds its way up the valleys. Ski resorts, hotels, and tourist shops bring their Swiss-German workers with them. Either way Romanche declines.

Italian may be a minority language in Switzerland but it is the majority language across the border. Radio, TV, newspapers, publishers, authors and editors keep Italian bubbling with new life. Italian films and TV flood Canton Ticino and the Italian-speaking communities of Graubünden. No external support enriches Romanche. The Romanche themselves manage to disagree on cultural attitudes and divide into three main written and seven main spoken variants, divisions so keenly felt that for years no Romanche appeared on Swiss bank notes – not because of official neglect, but because the Romanche could not agree how to spell 'Ten Swiss Francs'.

Minority provisions for Romanche speakers

This is the one area where official Switzerland recognizes that a minority needs special protection. In June 1983 the Federal Parliament passed the 'Federal Law concerning Contributions to Cantons Graubünden and Ticino for the promotion of their Cultures and Languages'. Article 1 stipulates explicitly that these contributions must go to the encouragement of the Rhaeto-Romanche language and culture and for the promotion of Italian culture both in the Italian-speaking valleys of Graubünden and in Canton Ticino itself. The *Lia Rumanscha*, the official representative of Romanche culture, has charge of the administration of funds and the obligation to report through the cantonal government to the federal department of the interior.

A chair for Romanche literature now exists at the University of Zurich and its first holder, the brilliant Iso Camartin, does his best to awaken his fellow Swiss to the plight of the linguistic minority on their doorstep. As he said to a group of Welsh writers at a conference a few years ago: 'there is a kind of cultural tolerance which reveals an ill-concealed affinity to contempt'. The problem is, as Professor Camartin shrewdly notes, that Romanche literature has only a past, no future. Its very vocabulary reflects the experiences of its speakers, their history as poor peasants in the high valleys of the upper Rhine. The language imposes by its very nature a kind of provinciality, and if the language does not do that, the readers soon will.

The 'new minorities'

If official Switzerland recognizes and protects its delicate linguistic minorities, it gives little or no protection to its hundreds of thousands of foreign workers. *Fremdarbeiter* or foreign workers come in three types: the largest group, the settled workers who have lived and worked in Switzerland long enough to have permanent residence (roughly 475,000), and the other two groups, those who cross the frontier daily to work in Switzerland but live in Germany, France or Italy, and those who cross the border on seasonal or annual permits. In April 1990 the two categories amounted to 268,904 persons with annual or seasonal permits and 169,139 who cross frontiers each day to work in Switzerland. In effect, Switzerland has no unemployment because it exports the unemployed by simply reducing the number of permits it gives for seasonal or annual work.

The numbers are large – and even larger when families of foreign workers are considered. The population of Switzerland in 1983 was 6,723,000 of whom 1,040,325 or 15.47% were aliens. Of these just under a third are Italians. This huge foreign population constitutes an underclass whose evolution promises to be the great social problem of the next generation.

For example, take the case of Giovanna M., born in Schaffhausen of Italian parents working in Switzerland. Giovanna grew up speaking Italian and Swiss-German without an accent in either. She went to Swiss schools and had Swiss training, but she has no Swiss rights. Since neither of her parents had Swiss nationality, she cannot claim it either. Indeed until recently even a Swiss mother could not pass nationality on to her offspring, and even now, if married to a non-Swiss, can only do so if the child is born in Switzerland.

Citizenship in Switzerland depends on membership of a local community. Every Swiss, regardless of where he or she may live, has a place of fundamental civic identity, where the register records his or her name. Generations may pass. The person may never have seen his 'home' but there on his or her passport is entered the name of the *Heimatort*, the place of his or her home. It sounds romantic until the case of Giovanna M. is considered.

Since Swiss communities have ultimate relief and welfare responsibilities for their 'citizens', ie. those registered, they have little incentive to add strangers to the list, still less the names of immigrant Italian children with lower-class backgrounds and origins in the Mezzogiorno. Some communities and cantons charge large sums for the privilege of registration. Recently in a village in central Switzerland the citizens attempted to prevent the children of an unpopular 'foreign' family applying for citizenship by arbitrarily raising the registration fee to the equivalent of £2000 per head. Since the same village had shortly before admitted a local doctor to citizenship for a fraction of that sum, the cantonal government intervened. The case is making its way to the federal court.

It is a cruel anomaly that allows, for example, refugee Bolivian tin millionaires to buy citizenship almost as soon as their expensive shoes touch the tarmac while Giovanna, born and bred Swiss, must be content to be a non-person in the Swiss community. But will she, and others like her, continue to accept the status quo?

The waves of migration washed over Switzerland in the 1950s and 1960s. By the 1970s it became clear that immigrants were there to stay. The children born of that generation have come of age. Many feel bitter about Switzerland where they may live and work but never vote. Some day that bitterness may explode. The author has repeatedly asked Swiss friends if the prospect does not alarm them but has found only a few who seem to be concerned.

Recently the problem of immigrants seeking asylum has stretched the patience of Swiss communities and led to sporadic outbursts of violence. It has not helped that these newest minorities, like Tamils, have brown skins. Here, in the face of these new minorities, the Swiss tend to try to shut them and the problem out.

Some lessons

This loose survey suggests that Switzerland has its share of the general problems that beset humanity but that in Switzerland, as always, they take peculiar forms. It may have no legislation to acknowledge the existence of most of its minorities, but it has them nonetheless. It also offers its peculiar beehive structure of democracy to those minorities which can be defined by residence.

Swiss communal democracy could provide the structures to cope with minority problems elsewhere in Europe, but for that to work the warring communities would have to accept the lesson the Swiss seem to have absorbed: let each village and community be as sovereign as it can be over as much public activity as possible. Keep responsibility near the base. Sometimes citizens will behave badly (as in the case of the charges for citizenship), but on the whole communal misbehaviour will cause less damage than that of national bad government.

Finally, give each community the right to defend its cultural identity. The citizens may hate their neighbours but they will have less incentive to take arms against them. These principles have made the protection of the minorities in Switzerland easier and much more peaceful.

Footnotes

[1] The author recalls an agreeable evening spent over large schooners of beer with a man who rejoiced in the romantic title of *Brunnenmeister*, master of the fountains, of a small central Swiss village. He explained that he had recently been appointed to this high office and that equipping himself and his firm had cost him thousands of Swiss francs. The job involved maintenance of drains and water supplies. When the author asked him if he had got the job through competition, he looked at him pityingly. 'But I am a Liberal. We have a three to two majority on the town council.' Did that mean that if the Conservatives got in at the next local election, he would be out, thousands of francs invested or not? 'But of course', he answered, now genuinely puzzled.

[2] The author's wife, who belongs to a large energetic Swiss family in Central Switzerland had never met a Swiss Protestant until the author introduced one to her – and that in spite of the fact that the main village where the older members of the family lived contained a sizable Protestant minority. Similarly the author knows of a village in Canton Luzern where housing officers reward party adherents and punish opponents in a manner worthy of Belfast, and can recall an evening when a Luzern conservative who was explaining party policy dropped to a whisper because people from 'the other side' had entered the pub.

[3] The author once met a distinguished French Swiss journalist who spoke English without an accent, but not a word of German, proper or Swiss German

THE NETHERLANDS
by Fred Grünfeld

Name: Koninkrijk der Nederlanden
Constitutional status: parliamentary democracy, constitutional monarchy
International organizations: UN, EC, CE, CSCE
Political/military alliances: NATO
Population: 15,036,000
Minorities: Frisians, 'new minorities' include Surinamese, Antilleans, Indonesians (including Moluccans), Moroccans, Turks, Greeks, Spanish, Portuguese, Yugoslavians.
Languages: Dutch
Religion: Catholic (one third), Protestant Churches (one third), others and no religious affiliation (one third)

The Netherlands population consists of many minority groups. In comparison with other plural societies, it is remarkable that these minorities are not of ethnic or national origin – with the sole exception of the Frisians in the north. The legitimacy of the central authority has never been questioned by the different ethnic, religious, regional or cultural groups in the country.

The historical background

The minorities were originally based on religious denominations. An ethnic aspect entered Dutch society relatively recently with the arrival of foreign workers and people from former Dutch colonies, often described as the 'new minorities'.

The latter came to the Netherlands over the past 20 years to seek employment, initially with the intention of staying only for a short period. The first of such groups of 'new minorities' came from the Mediterranean (mainly Spain, Portugal, Turkey and Morocco), and did not have Dutch nationality. The second wave arrived during the 1970s from the former Dutch colonies in Central and Latin America (Suriname and the Dutch West Indies); these have Dutch nationality. Combined, the members of the 'new minority' groups today form more than 6.5% of the Dutch population.

The 'old minorities' can be broadly divided into Catholics (38%), mainly located in the southern provinces of the Netherlands, and Protestants (31%), divided between members of Calvinist churches and the adherents to more liberal Protestant denominations. Although such distinctions derived from membership of religious groups, the implications of membership came to extend far beyond church-related affairs and as such played an important role in Dutch politics and society in general.

As a result of the peaceful co-existence of minority groups, the Netherlands acquired the reputation of being a relatively tolerant society. Because of this tradition, other groups, such as Huguenots and Jews, also chose to settle there. Freedom of religion and equal rights were – after an initial period – granted to them.

To what extent was this reputation for tolerance a sense of solidarity with other minorities, or was it merely the reflection of an attitude of indifference? It should not be forgotten that only 20% of the pre-war Dutch Jewish community survived World War II. In no other West European territory which was occupied by the Germans was the loss of Jewish lives so high as in the Netherlands.[1] It is beyond the scope of this report to analyse the causes of this tragedy, but – certainly from this example – there is doubt as to how far successful co-existence in plural societies stands the test of emergency situations when a society is occupied or under threat.

The 'old minority' groups and compromise politics

For decades – until the mid-1960s – political, social and cultural life in the Netherlands was described by the term 'pillarization' (*verzuiling*). (Another term for such denominational segregation is 'columnization'.) A 'pillar' consists of a conglomerate of sections of the population, who are united in a complex of organizations and institutions in society which are rooted in the same religion or ideology. The key question is how solid these confessional-political groups of the population were, and how a form of national political unity was achieved through which consensus could be reached.

The three main 'pillars' were the Catholics, the Protestants and the socialists: each with their connected political parties, trade unions, newspapers and broadcasting organizations, etc. The Catholics and Protestants also run the majority of all schools in the Netherlands, which are totally subsidized by the government. The liberals and conservatives never developed their own similar 'pillars', although they have connections with the employers' organization, and to a lesser degree with newspapers and broadcasting companies.[2]

Some insight can be gained into the solidarity of the interrelations within one 'pillar', together with the divisions between the pillars, by reference to some results of research conducted in 1964:

a) Catholics: 81% of the members of the NKV trade union, 76% of the listeners of the KRO broadcasting company, and 72% of the readers of the *Volkskrant/Tijd* newspaper voted for the KVP (the Catholic People's Party);

b) Protestants: 68% of the members of the CNV trade union, 72% of the listeners of the NCRV broadcasting company, and 95% of the readers of *Trouw* newspaper voted for the ARP (the Anti-Revolutionary Party) or the CHU (the Christian Historical Party);

c) Socialists: 78% of the members of the NVV trade union, 76% of the listeners of the VARA broadcasting company, and 68% of the readers of the *Vrije Volk/Parool* newspaper voted for the Pv/dA (the Labour Party).

After World War II the socialists did not envisage forming their own pillar, but hoped for a breakthrough by attracting members of different religious denominations. However, these efforts largely failed because the traditional confessional pillars offered stubborn resistance; for instance, in 1954 the Catholic bishops ordered members of the Catholic church not to join NVV or even to listen to the VARA or read a socialist newspaper.

Accordingly, the solidarity within the pillars remained strong, and cross-contacts were minimal – certainly at the level of the mass membership, although among the elite there were many more contacts between members of different pillars. There were, for example, a number of umbrella organizations (for instance, in socio-economic fields) in which all the pillars were represented. These played an important advisory role for the government, and such structures were necessary to counter the centrifugal tendencies of the 'pillarization'.

No political party of any one pillar obtained a majority of votes in the elections, and different political parties were therefore obliged to co-operate in coalition governments. The role of the political leaders necessarily had to be directed towards a policy of compromise. In this way they could maintain their position of power within their own group, and keep the groups separate while avoiding conflicts between them. In other words, dynamic political choices had to give way to a proportional distribution of power and resources, in order that 'everybody could be the boss in his own house while the house is paid for by the public purse'.

It is possible to identify several characteristics of this politics of compromise, including:

a) it was a practical, business-like policy, directed at obtaining concrete results;

b) in pragmatic acceptance or tolerance of another pillar, a kind of 'agreement to disagree' was reached: the political majority took account of the feelings of different minorities, and did not adopt a policy which offended the principal ideological views of these minorities, with sensitive decisions being taken only after consultation with those minorities;

c) key meetings between the leaders of the pillars took place when crises developed;

d) there was a 'just' proportional distribution of power and money;

e) a tendency to depoliticize developed, presenting politically sensitive issues as mere technical complexities;

f) a trend towards secrecy also evolved, in order that the elite could seek and find compromises, untroubled by popular interference;

g) the government came to be perceived as neutral, yet vested with a great deal of authoritative power.

It was central to this form of politics that the various constituencies trusted their respective leaders and held them in high esteem, and that they agreed with this policy of compromise in order to solve problems in a harmonious way by avoiding conflicts. This attitude, however, came to an end in the mid-1960s, for several reasons.

Democratization and politicization

In international politics a number of important developments took place which had a profound impact on political life in the Netherlands. Following the diminution of the Cold War, the bipolar world system was replaced by a more polycentral system, while Dutch perceptions of its most powerful ally, the USA, changed as a result of the latter's actions abroad (Vietnam) and at home (Watergate).

A growing awareness of the North-South dichotomy, accompanied in certain sectors of the population by admiration of the revolutionary heroes of the Third World and their ideals, resulted in broadening the previously somewhat narrow view of the national role in international politics. These factors not only resulted in more open discussion on Dutch foreign policy but also created conflicting views on domestic policy issues.

Strong economic growth in the 1950s and 1960s created new social tensions, as increasing numbers of people became more concerned about inequalities in society rather than absolute economic growth. The old social ties loosened and many young people created their own sub-culture. These developments led to demands for greater participation and democratization in many fields – expressed through, for example, the student revolts in and after 1968. The result was a challenge to authority and a decline in respect for political leaders.

This also led to polarization both within and among the political parties, and to the creation of single-issue groups in society. This emancipation of sectoral interests in turn caused the decay of internal loyalty within the pillars, and confessional parties began to lose support in the elections. By stressing their ideological differences during the election campaigns, political leaders found it increasingly difficult to form coalition cabinets, although the electoral system made such coalitions inevitable.

Nor was it possible to hold top-level meetings in secrecy, because the rank and file wanted to have a say in the decision-making process. The freedom of action of political leaders diminished markedly throughout the 1970s: grass-roots members of the political parties obtained greater power, and claimed a voice in major issues of decision-making, including the composition of the cabinet.

Furthermore, recent governments have had only small majorities in parliament, and their support has become even more unstable because, even within the political parties supporting the government, those members holding dissenting opinions became more vocal. Policy-making in the Netherlands became more interesting: clashes between government and parliament took place on many subjects such as abortion, socio-economic policies, the embargo on South Africa, the cruise missile issue, etc.

Increasingly the conflicts, on both domestic and foreign affairs, could be characterized as conflicts between the left and the right of the political spectrum. This trend has been reinforced because of the loss of power of the Catholic and Protestant pillars, which in reality disappeared as separate entities.

That of the Catholics – the largest minority in the Netherlands, with a central position in the Dutch political system which had to some extent completed their emancipation – was the first to crumble. Many of the new generation, especially among Catholics, broke with their religious community. The Catholic political party (KVP) shrank during the 1970s to half of its size in the 1950s. In 1980 it merged with the two other confessional parties (CHU, ARP) to form the Christian Democratic Appeal (CDA); the Catholic trade union merged with the socialist trade union eventually to form the Netherlands Trade Union Federation (FNV).

Of the Catholic newspapers, one ceased publication and the other became an important national newspaper of the left. Partly as a result, the new confessional party (CDA) lost its left-wing electorate and became more and more a conservative party. At the municipal elections of 1984 it lost its majority position in the predominantly Catholic south, and in some southern cities the Labour Party (PvdA) became the largest party for the first time.

Later the CDA stabilized and regained strength, once again becoming the major political party. It also kept its majority position in all Dutch coalition cabinets and its influence on policy-making did not diminish. On the contrary, the other political parties – Liberal and Labour – are presently adapting their political views to this confessional party, thus moving to the centre of the political spectrum. This development caused a remarkable falling away of their traditional electorate, especially that of the Labour Party which is seen as entering the 1990s without any ideological base. Thus 'depillarization' in the long run has had an enormous impact on the Labour Party which resulted in the loss of its traditional electorate.

Nevertheless the Netherlands still remains a country of minorities; and those in power continue to give due respect to the feelings and principal views of the other minorities, trying to avoid offending their sensitivities. If they do so – as happened over the deployment of the cruise missiles – they do so reluctantly: a number of the proponents of the final decision deplored that this decision had to be taken on the basis of a narrow majority.

The Frisians

The Frisians are the only indigenous linguistic minority in the Netherlands. They are based in the province of Friesland in the north-west of the Netherlands, which includes a number of islands. Of the 550,000 inhabitants, about 400,000 are Frisian-language speakers with possibly another 300,000 living outside the province. Many town dwellers speak 'town Frisian', a mixed dialect of Dutch and Frisian dating back to the 17th Century. Both the separate Frisian language and its culture were revived and nourished by the Frisian-language movement which took its modern form from the early 20th Century.

Friesland is unique among the 11 Dutch provinces in that the inhabitants are allowed to speak and write their own language as the second language, along with Dutch. Frisian has also been recognized as a medium of instruction since 1955 and in 1975 the Dutch government accepted a proposal that it be used in primary schooling and be made a compulsory study subject. The language is also studied at colleges and universities elsewhere in the Netherlands.

Frisians have a strong attachment to the Royal House of Orange, and therefore have never developed a separatist movement but remained loyal to the Kingdom of the Netherlands. Their cultural autonomy has been safeguarded. The Frisian cause has its own political party, which however won only 6.09% of the Frisian vote in the elections of the Frisian Provincial Council in March 1991. The foremost goal of this party was the maintenance of cultural autonomy, and it has shown no political ambitions beyond this aim.

The new minorities

In March 1991 there were 703,597 aliens registered in the Netherlands (4.68% of the population). The most conspicuous increase in their numbers occurred after 1960; this development was the result of the arrival of foreign workers – especially Turks and Moroccans – together with their families. The immigration of foreign workers has now virtually ceased, but dependants of those already in the country are still being admitted. Indeed it is now – in a declining economy – exclusively for purposes of family reunion that entry is granted.

The average fertility rate of non-Dutch women is over twice that of the overall average for Dutch women; an average of 5.1 children for Moroccans, 3.2 for Turks and 1.5 for Dutch. Furthermore, the death rate of non-Dutch residents is some three times lower than that of Dutch nationals, as a result of the relatively youthful age structure of the group. At the start of 1984, about 60% of the aliens had been living in the Netherlands for more than five years. These non-Dutch residents were entitled for the first time to participate in the municipal elections of 1986, both as voters and as candidates.

Apart from these groups, about 280,000 people of Suriname or other Caribbean origin (1.86% of the population) are resident in the Netherlands, which brings the total of the new minorities to 6.54%. Until Suriname's independence in 1975, the Surinamese were Dutch citizens and able to move freely between the two. Those Surinamese who resided in the Netherlands at the time of independence remained Dutch citizens; those in Suriname became Surinamese citizens. In practice, the division has not been as rigid as it might appear and Surinamese citizens can still enter the Netherlands, although with restrictions, while family reunion and resettlement are relatively easy.

An increasing growth in the numbers of these groups can be expected in the future. For example, when the South Moluccans arrived in 1951 they numbered 13,000, and had risen to 40,000 by 1989. Furthermore, they tend be concentrated in certain areas such as Amsterdam where, in 1991, 9.7% of the total population are people of Suriname and Caribbean origin, and 8.7% have a Turkish and Mediterranean background, and these groups constituted 38.13% of the Amsterdam population in the age group of 17 years of age and under.

When the foreign workers first arrived, it was expected that they would stay for a short period. By the beginning of the 1980s, however, it had become clear that this was not the case. The permanent nature of the settlement had changed the Netherlands into a multicultural society.

In response the government formulated a policy: the official aim was to integrate the foreigners into Dutch society, while assuring that they could maintain their own identity. At the same time it was recognized that the similarities between the minority groups were greater than the differences among them. These similarities were identified as structural, having been caused by their position in Dutch society. Their level of education is low; their housing situation is poor; their unemployment level is at least twice that of the other inhabitants of the Netherlands.

In mid-1987, unemployment levels for various groups were as follows: Dutch 13%; Surimanese 27%; Antilleans 23%; Turks 44%; Moroccans 42%. Moveover, in comparison with the situation as measured in 1983, the position of the new minorities has worsened. Using 100 as the 1983 index, Dutch unemployment had decreased to 88 while those of other groups had increased: Antilleans 138; Surinamese 137; Turks 114; Moroccans 126.

Despite the stated policy objective of positive action for minorities, the reality is that their position is worsening, as demonstrated in unemployment figures for Amsterdam city, where it is obvious that minorities in the age 18-64 are affected more severely by unemployment than the Dutch.

The reorganization of Dutch industry in the 1980s caused

predominantly the loss of jobs of those with a low level of education. About 75% of the members of the new minorities had received only primary education, whereas the same is true for only 14% of the Dutch male population. There is an urgent need for a greater effort to mobilize education and skills training in order to overcome the alarming problems of unemployment among the new minorities.

Amsterdam – population and unemployment

	Total population	0-17 years	18-64 years	unemploy -ment
Surinamese	8.3%	15.14%	7.14%	10.57%
Antilleans	1.4%	2.36%	1.32%	2.59%
Turks	3.5%	7.31%	2.9%	4.89%
Moroccans	5.2%	13.32%	3.79%	5.84%
Other aliens	7.7%	8.56%	8.33%	7.63%
Dutch	74.0%	53.4%	76.23%	68.47%
Total	702,731	117,008	474,311	65,309

Figures from January 1990, total population figure from January 1991.

Some lessons

Extensive research has shown that systematic racial discrimination did not and does not exist in the Netherlands, even though a growing number of racial incidents have been identified. Nevertheless, there is a wide degree of consensus within Dutch society that discrimination is totally unacceptable.

One possible explanation for this consensus may be the political culture of Dutch society. Because of the old 'pillarization', in which the internal sovereignty of each section of society ('a boss in his own house') was accepted, assimilation was not forced upon the new minorities. It was not seen as necessary for them to give up their own identity in order to integrate into Dutch society, a society in which strong feelings of nationalism have been markedly absent.

Nevertheless, in a declining economy, competition among people is sharper and more direct. This competition can arouse prejudices, which however do not always entail discriminatory behaviour. There is an awareness of the existence of these problems in Dutch society, which in itself is a step towards overcoming them. It is therefore to be hoped that co-existence between the Dutch and these new minorities will still remain successful.

Footnotes

[1] In 1940, there were 128,00 Dutch Jews; 107,000 were deported to concentration camps, of whom 5200 survived. The loss of about 101,800 – about 80% of the pre-war Dutch Jewish community – should be compared with the loss in Belgium of about 28%, in Luxembourg of about 15%, in France of about 19%, in Germany itself about 74%, in Denmark of 1%, and in Italy of about 15%. (In some countries figures differ as to the number of Jews living there before the war).

[2] Radio and television time in the Netherlands is distributed according to the adherents of the different broadcasting companies, and is paid for by the government.

An CSCE expert meeting on minorities was held in Geneva in July 1991. It was sponsored by the Swiss Government, in part as a special effort to promote minority issues during its 700th Anniversary year, but also to give special focus to the new concentration on minorities in Europe, expressed by the CSCE participating states at previous meetings in Copenhagen and Paris. The meeting was given special poignancy by the tragic drama unfolding in Yugoslavia.

Governments were urged to consider positive and practical recommendations on minorities. A report from the CSCE meeting was adopted on the last day of the expert meeting. The single most significant act of the meeting was to adopt a change in the concept of the sovereign national state. The report states:

Issues concerning national minorities, as well as compliance with international obligations and commitments concerning the rights of persons belonging to them, are matters of legitimate international concern and consequently do not constitute exclusively an internal affair of the respective State.

The meeting did not elaborate on the standards set in previous CSCE documents. However, it reaffirmed previous CSCE commitments and, more importantly, ways of implementing those commitments, listing different measures to monitor implementation.

The key words for the implementation of the commitments are: effective participation in public affairs; appropriate democratic participation of persons belonging to national minorities or their representatives in decision-making or consultative bodies; resolving specific problems through dialogue between States, and between States and persons belonging to national minorities, based on a free flow of information and ideas between all parties.

On minority participation in public affairs:

Aware of the diversity and varying constitutional systems among them, which make no single approach necessarily generally applicable, the participating States note with interest that positive results have been obtained by some of them in an appropriate manner by, *inter alia*:

advisory and decision-making bodies in which minorities are represented, in particular with regard to education, culture and religion;

● elected bodies and assemblies of national minority affairs;

● local and autonomous administration, as well as autonomy on a territorial basis, including the existence of consultative, legislative and executive bodies chosen through free and periodic elections;

● self-administration by a national minority of aspects concerning its identity in situations where autonomy on a territorial basis does not apply;

● decentralized or local forms of government;

● bilateral and multilateral agreements regarding national minorities;

● for persons belonging to national minorities, provisions of adequate types and levels of education in their mother tongue with due regard to the number, geographical settlement patterns and cultural traditions of national minorities;

● funding the teaching of minority language to the general public, as well as the inclusion of minority languages in teacher-training institutions, in particular in regions inhabited by persons belonging to national minorities;

● in cases where instruction in a particular subject is not provided in their territory in the minority language at all levels, taking the necessary measures to find means of recognizing diplomas issued abroad for a course of study completed in that language;

● creation of government research agencies to review legislation and disseminate information related to equal rights and non-discrimination;

● provision of financial and technical assistance to persons belonging to national minorities who so wish to exercise their right to establish and maintain their own educational, cultural and religious institutions, organizations and associations;

● governmental assistance for addressing local difficulties relating to discriminatory practices (eg. a citizens' relations service);

● encouragement of grassroots community relations efforts between neighbouring communities sharing borders, aimed at helping to prevent local tensions from arising and address conflicts peacefully should they arise; and

● encouragement of the establishment of permanent mixed commissions, either inter-State or regional, to facilitate continuing dialogue between the border regions concerned.

● The participating States are of the view that these or other approaches, individually or in combination, could be helpful in improving the situation of national minorities on their territories.

On the free flow of information and exchange of ideas:

● They will take effective measures to promote tolerance, understanding, equality of opportunity and good relations between individuals of different origins within their country.

● In access to the media, they will not discriminate against anyone based on ethnic, cultural, linguistic or religious grounds. They will make information available that will assist the electronic mass media in taking into account, in their programmes, the ethnic, cultural, linguistic and religious identity of national minorities.

● They reaffirm that establishment and maintenance of unimpeded contacts among persons belonging to a national minority, as well as contacts across frontiers by persons belonging to a national minority with persons with whom they share a common ethnic or national origin, cultural heritage or religious belief, contributes to mutual understanding and promotes good-neighbourly relations.

● They therefore encourage trans-frontier co-operation arrangements on a national, regional and local level, inter alia, on local border crossings, the preservation of and visits to cultural and historical monuments and sites, tourism, the improvement of traffic, the economy, youth exchange, the protection of the environment and the establishment of regional commissions.

● They will also encourage the creation of informal working arrangements (e.g. workshops, committees, both within and between the participating States) where national minorities live, to discuss issues of, exchange experiences on, and present proposals on, issues related to national minorities.

On the implementation of CSCE commitments:

● The participating States note that appropriate CSCE mechanisms may be of relevance in addressing questions relating to national minorities. Further, they recommend that third meeting of the Conference on the Human Dimension of the CSCE consider expanding the Human Dimension Mechanism. They will promote the involvement of individuals in the protection of their rights, including the rights of persons belonging to national minorities.

● With a view to improve their information about actual situation of national minorities, the participating States will, on a voluntary basis distribute, through the CSCE Secretariat, information to other participating States about the situation of national minorities in their respective territories, as well as statements of national policy in that respect.

Select Bibliography

There is extensive literature in many languages on the situations of specific European minority groups and on the legal and constitutional provisions relating to them. Resources which deal with some of the legal provisions relating to minorities, and which are available through the Minority Rights Group include:

FAWCETT, James, *The International Protection of Minorities*, MRG Report, 1979.
PALLEY, Claire, *Constitutional Law and Minorities*, MRG Report, 1978.
MINORITY RIGHTS GROUP, (Ed.), *World Directory of Minorities*, Longmans/St James, 1989.
MINORITY RIGHTS GROUP, (Ed.), *Minority Rights in Europe: Policies and Practices in CSCE Participating States*, (Report on the Leningrad Minority Rights Conference, USSR, 2-4 June 1991), MRG Conference Report, 1991.
SKUTNABB-KANGAS, Tove, *Language, Literacy and Minorities*, MRG Report, 1990.
THORNBERRY, Patrick, *Minorities and Human Rights Law*, MRG Report, 1991.

About Minority Rights Group Reports

The Minority Rights Group began publishing in 1970. Over two decades and ninety titles later, MRG's series of reports are widely recognized internationally as authoritative, accurate and objective documents on the rights of minorities worldwide.

Over the years, subscribers to the series have received a wealth of unique material on ethnic, religious, linguistic and social minorities. The reports are seen as an important reference by researchers, students, campaigners and provide readers all over the world with valuable background data on many current affairs issues.

Around six reports are published every year. Each title, expertly researched and written, is approximately 30 pages and 20,000 words long and covers a specific minority issue.

Recent titles in our report series include:

Europe
Romania's Ethnic
   Hungarians
Refugees in Europe

Africa
The Sahel
Somalia

Middle East
Beduin of the Negev
The Kurds

Southern Oceans
Maori of Aotearoa-New Zealand
The Pacific: Nuclear Testing
   and Minorities

General
Language, Literacy
   and Minorities

Asia
Afghanistan
Bangladesh

Americas
Maya of Guatemala

If you have found this report informative and stimulating, and would like to learn more about minority issues, please do subscribe to our report series. It is only with the help of our supporters that we are able to pursue our aims and objectives – to secure justice for disadvantaged groups around the world.

We currently offer a reduced annual rate for individual subscribers – please ring our Subscription Desk on +44 (0)71 978 9498 for details. Payment can be easily made by MasterCard or Visa over the telephone or by post.

All enquiries to: Sales Department
The Minority Rights Group
379 Brixton Road
London
SW9 7DE
United Kingdom

Customers in North America wishing to purchase copies of our reports should contact:

Cultural Survival
53 Church Street
Cambridge
MA 02138
USA